You'll
Never
Make
Love
in This
Town
Again

by

ROBIN
LIZA
LINDA
and
TIFFANY

as told to

Jennie Louise Frankel,
Terrie Maxine Frankel

and

Joanne Parrent

Preface by
Dr. Lois Lee

Editor's Introduction by
Joanne Parrent

DOVE
BOOKS

The publisher of this book has made every effort to insure the accuracy of all material contained in *You'll Never Make Love In This Town Again*. Each of the four contributors to the book, Robin, Liza, Linda, and Tiffany, were given polygraph tests by an outside, independent firm to determine the veracity of their stories. All were certified by the examiners as having told the truth. In addition, all of the contributors' accounts were verified by Peter Maheu of Maheu Associates, a private investigation firm, and the manuscript was reviewed twice by Louis Petrich, Esq., an attorney specializing in First Amendment law at Leopold, Petrich and Smith, to determine the validity of legal claims. Although two names have been changed, all of the information contained herein is, to the best of the editors' and publisher's knowledge, accurate.

ISBN 0-7871-0404-3

Printed in the United States of America

Dove Books
301 North Cañon Drive
Beverly Hills, CA 90210

Distributed by Penguin USA

Text design and layout by Folio Graphics
Jacket design and layout by Rick Penn-Kraus

Photo credits: p. 1: Bill Rich Photography
               p. 21: Courtesy of the author
               p. 136: Courtesy of the author
               p. 137: Jim Pickerell / WESTLIGHT
               p. 207: Jennifer Howard

First Printing: December 1995

10   9   8   7   6   5   4   3   2   1

Contents

Preface • *vii*

Editor's Introduction • *xi*

Robin • *1*

Liza • *21*

Linda • *137*

Tiffany • *207*

Preface

Millions of women work as prostitutes in the United States. Whether they work on the streets, from parlors, their homes, or telephones, prostitutes all have something in common; they are victims in a conspiracy of silence to conceal the identities of the men who pay them for sex. Some experts argue prostitutes are paid for sex, for humiliation or degradation, but the real reason they get paid is for their silence—to provide their customers with confidentiality. In exchange, these women assume full responsibility for their work—they are incarcerated, criminalized, and blamed by society for providing sexual services to some of the most powerful men in the world. Customers come from all social classes and ethnic groups. Laborers, truck drivers, and salesmen are common customers for the street prostitute. But in the police "trick task forces" where female officers are used as decoys to arrest the customer, there are almost always one policeman and one attorney, among the other occupations. Attorneys are the most common of the professions. But there are rabbis, priests, ministers, movie stars, producers, diplomats, you name it. Typically the customers are seventy-five percent white and ninety-five percent married.*

---

*All statistics cited herewith are as per *People v. Hakim*, case 687994, Los Angeles Municipal Court, Van Nuys, California.

There are no accurate official numbers on how many women work as prostitutes in the United States. The only numbers available are police reports which are largely limited to street and parlor prostitution. The stigma attached to prostitution keeps women uncounted. Women lose status for their involvement in prostitution and men gain status, at least "among the boys."

In any event, the number of men who pay women for sex far outnumber the number of women working as prostitutes. Yet the enforcement of the laws designed to deter prostitution are unequally enforced against the prostitute. When a male vice officer works on the streets attempting to arrest a prostitute, he may arrest four or five prostitutes a night. When a female police officer is placed on the corner and men come up to solicit her, she is able to arrest sixty or seventy customers a night.

In Los Angeles, courts have refused to find unequal this enforcement of prostitution law where ten percent of prostitution arrests are customers, thirty percent male prostitutes, and sixty percent female prostitutes. The courts limit the interpretation of "unequal enforcement" to a male-female ratio adding the number of male prostitutes to male customers in order to find constitutionality, with no regard to the fact that ninety percent of all arrests are prostitutes and ten percent are customers.

Prostitution is a social problem, but the current treatment of prostitution treats the female as a criminal subjecting her to arrest and incarceration. In fact, seventy percent of the women now serving time for felonies were first arrested for prostitution.

California has some of the toughest prostitution

laws. For the first conviction a judge has discretion in sentencing, but the second conviction is a mandatory forty-five days in County Jail, and the third conviction is a mandatory ninety days in County Jail. The maximum sentence is five hundred dollars and six months in jail.

Customers are rarely arrested, and if they are they are usually subjected to mere fines.

Women who prostitute themselves suffer a severe social stigma. They are isolated from family, non-prostitute friends, and boyfriends. It is not a wonder that many use drugs or alcohol to cope with their isolation and loneliness or fall victim to the ploys of male pimps and hustlers.

The customer just moves on to a younger, prettier woman to meet his needs of immediate gratification.

Here, the stories of Liza, Linda, and Tiffany are not unusual for women who find themselves trapped in a lifestyle of prostitution. Their backgrounds do not differ significantly from other women involved or not involved in prostitution, but the values they've internalized and the weight they've attributed to their beauty, reinforced by a society that emphasizes youth and beauty, entraps them in a world with access to rich, famous, and powerful men.

You'll Never Make Love In This Town Again breaks the code of silence—the conspiracy—and tells the stories of young women who found themselves trapped in a lie. Simply put, their problematic lifestyle, if it didn't involve sex, would be treated as an ordinary social problem capable of remedy.

Each woman is trapped by a societal conspiracy to blame the victim and diminish the prostitution problem by making prostitution a psychological problem lodged in the individual prostitute's head rather than look at the whole problem.

Why not open the books of madams and look at the customers and attempt to figure out a solution? Let's put the players on the table and look at this problem to find solutions rather than discard the lives of young women who seek occupations in which they meet the needs of some of the most powerful men in America.

Robin, Liza, Linda and Tiffany have taken that first brave step in trying to end the oppression and conspiracy of silence—to name their counterparts.

Some of us have a lot to learn. These women have a lot to forget.

—Dr. Lois Lee
Founder and Executive Director
Children of the Night

Children of the Night is a non-profit, tax exempt organization dedicated to rescuing children ages 11–17 from prostitution.

For more information please write or call:

Children of the Night
P.O. Box 4343
Hollywood, CA 90078
818-908-4474

Editor's Introduction

Los Angeles is a place where rich and powerful men get away with, among other things, murder. This book is about some of the other things they get away with.

At the corner of Civic Center Drive and Beverly Boulevard in Beverly Hills, the famous "Bunny" symbol of Playboy Enterprises is displayed proudly on a large modern office building. Only a few miles to the east is a high-rise on the corner of Wilshire and La Cienega, formerly the Great Western Savings building, which in large letters tells us that the new owners are "Larry Flynt Publications, Inc.," the publisher of *Hustler* magazine. The message is loud and clear as you drive around the Westside of Los Angeles—exploiting women's bodies is a booming business. These "Private Diaries" tell the stories of four women and the many Hollywood men they've encountered. But the revelations in this book, as stunning as many of them may be, represent only the tip of the iceberg of the sexist culture not only here in Los Angeles, but throughout the world.

Editing this book made me recall some of my own close encounters as a young women new to Hollywood. When I first moved to Los Angeles in the late seventies, it was hard not to love it. The sunshine, the ocean, the friendly people, the pinks and greens, the palm trees were all delightful to someone from the cold, drab Midwest. It didn't take long, however, for me to see another side of Los Angeles.

In the course of my work then, as a documentary filmmaker, I met a woman who told me her name was "Lottie Da." We immediately liked each other, though we were from opposite worlds. I considered myself an intellectual and a feminist. I spent my spare time organizing Hollywood parties to raise money for the Equal Rights Amendment. Lottie, as she proudly told me, was a call girl, a member of the hooker's union, COYOTE (Call Off Your Old Tired Ethics) founded by prostitute Margo St. John. And Lottie didn't go to Hollywood parties to raise money for the ERA—she went to work.

Lottie was filled with energy and enthusiasm. She didn't look like a prostitute, I thought. But then I asked myself what does a prostitute look like, after all? Perhaps her lipstick was a little redder than that of other women I knew. She was short, blonde, cute, fairly large busted, and she had large eyes, which at times seemed so sad and vulnerable. Lottie and I had a mutual interest in old films from the thirties and forties and in feminist issues. She would call from time to time, or come over and we'd talk. Once I invited her to a wrap party I gave for a documentary film about Norman Cousins that I had just directed. She came with a friend, also a prostitute, and seemed very grateful to me for inviting her, for no other reason than the fact that she was my friend. Usually, when Lottie was invited to a party it was to work it.

I was unprepared, however, when Lottie came by one day and asked me to help her out. She really needed a girl to "service" a friend of a regular client of hers. I could make five hundred dollars for only a few hours with him. Would I help her out? I smiled and told her no, I didn't want to. "How do you know you won't like it until you try it?" she countered. I don't know how I knew. My life had taught me. My parents probably deserve some credit. Undoubtedly, it was also due to my years in the Women's Movement, protesting women being treated as "sex objects." Whatever, Lottie didn't convince me to turn a trick that night and she never asked again.

Thinking back on that experience, I realize that if even I had the opportunity to become a hooker—a small-busted, brown-haired intellectual who usually wears jeans and very little make-up—then that opportunity was certainly available to a large portion of the young women in L.A., particularly those who might have had more of the "look" that men desired—larger breasts, blonde hair—as well as women who might have been more desperate for money than I was.

And Lottie's offer wasn't the only opportunity I would get to sell my body—for money or promised reward—in Hollywood. A year or so later, I was coming out of the Writers' Guild building when James Toback, a writer-director, (*The Gambler*, *Bugsy*) approached me, introduced himself, and asked if I was an actress. I said I had studied acting (I had started to write dramatic films now and thought studying acting would be helpful). He asked me if I was free for lunch. He wanted to talk to me about a role in a script he had just written. He thought I would be perfect for it. How many young women in Hollywood have heard that line? And how many fall for it every day (see Tiffany's story about producer, Don Simpson, on page 220 for more on this). I fell for it and agreed to have lunch with him.

At lunch, he asked me a "philosophical" question—would I sleep with someone for a million dollars? I later learned that this question preoccupies many men in Hollywood—the glamorized male-fantasy film *Indecent Exposure* was certainly a product of this widespread preoccupation. I was also later to hear the joke that when a woman answers "yes" to the million dollar question, then the guy says, "Well, will you sleep with me for five dollars?" Indignant, the woman says, "NO! I'm not a whore!" He smiles and, in typical Hollywood deal-making style, says "We already established that you're a whore. Now, we're just negotiating about the price."

Back to my lunch with Toback, I didn't take the bait. I told him I wouldn't sleep with a guy I didn't want to sleep with even for a million dollars. I wondered what this stupid question had to do with his script. Nothing, it turned out. But he did ask me to read the script he'd written and meet with him later. It had to be today because he was going back to New York tomorrow. That bait I took. I read the script. It was about a young, innocent girl from the midwest (which I was) who became a model and got caught up in an international plot to trap a terrorist who was obsessed with models.

I met Toback again later that afternoon. He asked me to go with him while he stopped by to see his agent, Jeff Berg, at International Creative Management (ICM). Toback told me I was perfect for the lead in this movie. If the studio wouldn't agree to let me play the lead, he promised, then I could at least have the role of the second female lead, another model from the midwest. Toback introduced me to Jeff Berg and Jeff asked me what I thought of Toback's script.

As I sat in the meeting, I imagined a career for myself like Sam Shepard's—I'd still write, but I'd also act. After we left Jeff Berg's office, I agreed to go back to Toback's house to "run lines" from the script with him. It wasn't long, however, before this "audition" became more like a scene from a soft-porn movie. Toback suddenly grabbed my thigh and stuck his other hand into his pants, clutching his little hard thing, moaning and pulling it out. I jumped up and told him I was leaving. He reluctantly put his penis back in his pants, apologized, and then tried to get my sympathy by telling me that he was sexually abused as a child by an older man. I suggested that he see a therapist and was soon out of there, grateful that he hadn't tried to use force.

I went home and called my friend, Joan Hackett, a wonderful actress who died a few years later from ovarian cancer. Joan went ballistic when she heard what happened.

"Toback is a total sleaze bag!" roared Joan. "You have to report him to the Directors' Guild. You have to call Jeff Berg and tell him what happened!" She was even more furious than I was because, as an actress, she knew that what had happened to me happened to young aspiring actresses all the time. She knew how powerless they felt because, unlike me, they didn't have the Sam Shepard fantasies—acting was their only dream and they were more vulnerable to men like Toback.

I did call the Directors' Guild and, as far as I know, they never did anything about my complaint. Hopefully, they would today, since this was years before the country's awareness of sexual harassment was awakened by Anita Hill. I also called Jeff Berg. He was flabbergasted when I told him what had happened with Toback. "Why are you telling me this?" he asked, very irritated. "Because he's your client and his behavior is wrong. You can stop him from doing this to other women." Jeff Berg was speechless. He apparently had never had a call like this before.

Two minutes later I got a call from Toback. He whined, "Why didn't you call me rather than Jeff?" He had said he was sorry, he reminded me. I told him that what he did was a disgusting form of sexual harassment and, if he wasn't held accountable, he would just do it to the next woman who came along. Unfortunately, I'm sure he did anyway.

The dust had barely settled on the Toback episode when I got a call from Warren Beatty. When I asked, he insisted that Toback didn't give him my number, but that he had gotten it from Ed Asner's office (that seemed plausible at the time since I had just worked on a documentary film with Asner). After reading Liza's experience with Beatty in this book (on page 97), however, I now figure that he and Toback had some kind of bet going about whether Warren could get me into bed. Or, perhaps, as Bill Stadiem, the author of the biography of Heidi Fleiss' mentor, Madam Alex, suggested when I later told him the story, Toback was probably pimping for Beatty, finding women for him in return for favors from Beatty.

Liza's story about Beatty and mine share some common elements, and, thankfully, some differences. Warren's pursuit of me also went on for some time and it had the same obsessive quality. I first agreed to meet him out of curiosity, but his boyish shyness, his flattery, his promises, and the fact that he cooked for me kept me going back a few more times. Unlike Liza, fortunately, perhaps because I was older than she at the time and more cynical about men, I never believed most of what Warren said and didn't let my emotions or fantasies get involved. He may have been a good actor, but not good enough to hide the fact that his constant attention and phone calls were designed only to get me into bed. I was more amused by the game than taken in. What he enjoyed about me, I think, was that I would make fun of him and call him on his act. It also didn't take long before I started hearing similar Warren Beatty stories from other women he had pursued. Hundreds, perhaps thousands of young women in Hollywood during that period had encounters with this master womanizer, and his game was starting to get around.

The last time I was at Warren's house he had already moved on to new pursuits, but he invited me up to show him a documentary film I had just finished on sexual harassment on the job. It was a pre-Anita Hill film that was made for television and for training programs in an attempt to sensitize people to the problem of sexual harassment. After watching the film, Warren and I sparred a bit on the subject, and then he went to the projection room to get the film for me. His date for the evening, actress Barbara Hershey, had arrived in the meantime and had been standing in the doorway watching us discuss the film. When he left the room, she said to me, "Have you known him for a long time?" I said, "Not really, why?" "Because the way you stand up to him," she replied, as if in awe that I had said anything but 'yes Warren' to him, "I just thought you had known him a long time."

I was amused at the time, but later disturbed, particularly as I worked on this book. Why do women feel they shouldn't "stand up to" or assert their independent thoughts, feelings, and emotions to rich, famous, or powerful men? We *can* stand up to them, but too often, as in several of the stories in this book, we don't. Sadly, as this book reveals, not asserting ourselves or being "star struck" may benefit the famous man, but it usually only brings pain to the woman involved.

I was honored to work on this book because it exposes men who routinely use and abuse vulnerable, insecure young women in Hollywood. It is also a strong plea from these four women to other young women to stand up to men, to refuse to do things they don't feel comfortable doing, to keep their dignity and integrity—and it doesn't mince words about what is likely to happen if they don't.

I personally was spared from the worst of the Hollywood mill that grinds up young women and churns them out, because I was a well-educated feminist before I moved here and because I had friends like Joan Hackett who warned me about men like James Toback and Warren Beatty. Liza, Linda, and Tiffany weren't as lucky as I. But their stories, and Robin's introductory story, can be for other women who come to Hollywood with stars in their eyes; the same kind of warning I got from Joan: "Don't let them get away with this."

I write this now only a few days after the verdict in the O.J. Simpson trial. This book recounts a number of horrifying stories of men debasing women, hurting them physically and emotionally, and destroying their already fragile sense of self. The line between the sexual degradation of women in some of these stories and other forms of male violence and abuse—from sexual harassment, to verbal and emotional abuse, to wife battering, rape, mutilation, and even murder—is only one of degree. It all stems from the same sense of entitlement that many men have towards women's bodies.

I was outraged at the verdict and at the Simpson jurors, particularly the women, one of whom said that the domestic violence evidence in the trial was a "waste of time." I can only hope that those jurors are part of a dwindling minority of uninformed people. I hope that the courage of Robin, Liza, Linda, and Tiffany in coming forward with their stories will be rewarded, that this book will make a difference for other women, and that women will begin to say no to all forms of abuse. I hope that both women and men who are angered by the injustice that Nicole Brown Simpson and women like her receive in the courts will look at where the escalating violence begins—with the small demeaning acts, the vicious put-downs and threats, the slaps, the loveless fucks, the drugged-out debauches, the toilet sex, the sado-masochism, the buying and selling of women like highly-paid slaves, and the desire by some men, who are not exposed and stopped, for control and power over women. If we don't begin to see these connections, rich, powerful, and unethical men will continue to destroy the hopes, the dreams, and the spirits of too many beautiful and vulnerable young women—and they will even continue to get away with murder.

—Joanne Parrent
Los Angeles, California
October, 1995

Robin

Robin

HEIGHT:	*5'8"*
HAIR:	*Blonde*
EYES:	*Blue*
WEIGHT:	*120*
PROFESSION:	*Actress*
BORN:	*Hollywood, California*
HOBBIES:	*Tennis, reading, water sports, working out, and writing*
EDUCATION:	*University High School*
FIRST SEXUAL EXPERIENCE:	*At fifteen, with an eighteen-year-old classmate.*
GOALS AND DESIRES:	*To remarry and have children and live a relatively normal life.*
SEXUAL FANTASY:	*I don't have any left.*
DRUGS:	*Cocaine*
HAPPIEST MEMORY:	*My agent telling me I have a role on a prime-time evening show.*
WORST EXPERIENCE:	*Helplessly watching my sister's life being taken over by drugs.*
SEX PARTNERS:	*Lorenzo Lamas, Gary Busey, and more.*

THE DIARIES

For the Record

*P*eople are always struck by the amazing number of beautiful young girls they see around Beverly Hills and Hollywood. Everywhere they look there are gorgeous, long-legged, buxom, small-waisted, thin-hipped women wearing sexy clothing. Women flock here from around the world for acting roles and modeling assignments, and it doesn't take a rocket scientist to figure out there is a lot of competition for these jobs. Casting directors know this, producers know this, and con men know this. There are some pretty smooth talkers in Hollywood, waiting to exploit naive young women. They'll convince these girls that they can help them with their careers, when they can't or won't. Or they'll swear they love them when they don't. When these beautiful young women fall into the traps these men set and use their bodies to get ahead, it doesn't work, no matter how much the guy might say or imply that it will. The consequences, unfortunately, may be far more devastating than just failure to reach a career goal. I saw terrible things happen to my sister and to some of my friends. I count myself lucky enough to have been spared the worst of those experiences.

I have dated or met socially many influential men in Hollywood: Michael Fuchs of HBO, Academy Award-winning actor Gary Busey; my ex-fiance, Lorenzo Lamas; film mogul Jon Peters, and many more. None has ever helped me with my career. I have known some of the most powerful executives and deal-makers in this town, and the truth is that no matter how much they complimented my body or sexual skills, they were not there for me career-wise.

Of course, there are people with power in Hollywood who are genuinely looking for new talent. But they usually offer to help you when you meet them professionally, or at least not in a romantic or sexual context. Roseanne and Tom Arnold were two people who were helpful to me, and I met them through a social contact. Jack Nicholson also got me a small part in a movie, but I met him through my friendship with his daughter, Jennifer.

Recently a male friend told me about a very A-list Hollywood party he had just attended. He said he was the only person there whom he didn't recognize. He was talking with a group of men when he heard a powerful, well-known producer say, "Let's face it. The reason we all came here was to meet beautiful women and get laid." Indeed, that may be the case for many men who have come to Hollywood. They become successful agents, studio executives, or producers and make a lot of money—in between episodes of meeting beautiful women and getting laid. But the beautiful women who come here dreaming of their names in lights face a much different challenge. Meeting a rich, handsome guy and getting laid doesn't help. Hollywood is a boys' club, and the dreams that get fulfilled here are mostly male fantasies. So any girl who thinks she can sleep around to get ahead in Hollywood, just plan on getting fucked. That's all you can count on.

GROWING UP

101 Acts of Love

I grew up in a show-business family, but not a wealthy or famous one. My mother is a top model and my father a commercial director as well as a director of early soft-porn films that would be more like Rated-R films now. When I was a young girl, we moved to a big new house in Westwood. Soon after we arrived in the new neighborhood, I was invited to a birthday party for one of my classmates. At the party, the mother of my little friend asked me, "What does your daddy do?" I told her that he directed films. She naturally asked, "What has he directed?" "*101.*" I answered. Her face lit up. "*101 Dalmations!*" she exclaimed, "We all love that film." She went around the party and told everyone that my dad directed *101 Dalmations*. In actually, the film my father directed was a porno film called *101 Act of Love*. I didn't know then what "dalmations" meant, but I figured it was just another term for "acts of love." Later, when my friend's mother drove me home, she was still impressed with my father's credit. "Didn't you just love your father's movie?" she asked. "I couldn't see it," I

7

replied matter-of-factly. Surprised, she asked me why. "Because it's about people making love," I told her. "What?" She seemed confused. *101 Acts of Love*," I explained. "It's about people making love."

I was dropped off at home that day and that was the last I saw of that little girl or most of the other little girls in the neighborhood. But it didn't matter to me at the time; we were always considered the eccentric family wherever we lived. Now we were Westwood's "Addams Family." We were a close family and a dysfunctional one. In my early childhood my father was an alcoholic, and my mother, although loving, was very involved in her career and frequently had to travel, so she wasn't around much to raise or discipline the children.

There were three of us kids: my older brother, Don, my younger sister Liza, and me. As we grew older, everyone thought Liza was much more beautiful than me. She would be the star my dad predicted. Indeed, Liza was and still is extraordinarily beautiful. At the time it kind of hurt to not be thought of as quite as beautiful as my sister. But now I can look back and be grateful. Perhaps not thinking I was all that beautiful gave me more self-esteem in other areas. I'm not sure. But Hollywood, as Liza will acknowledge, basically ate her up and spit her out. Hollywood may have wounded me, but my beautiful younger sister ended up on the critical list.

I wanted to be an actress even though I knew I wasn't as pretty as my sister. I took acting very seriously and from a young age went to acting classes. I started doing commercials and B-grade movies when I was fifteen. Several times a week I would take the bus from our house in Westwood to my acting classes in the heart of Hollywood. When I was nineteen I met my future husband, Mark Slotkin, a successful business-man who was twenty years older than me. He thought it wasn't safe for me to be taking the bus to the sleazy neighborhood where I took my acting class—he wanted his limousine driver to take me instead. I refused the offer. "I like taking the bus," I told him. "That's where I get characters." Still worried, Mark told his driver to follow the bus and then follow me on my way from the bus stop to class. With Mark's limo always lurking around, I finally relented and began to ride back and forth to acting class in a limo. I made a big splash in class. That was the beginning of my journey through the glamorous Hollywood high life.

From our first date on, Mark and I fought over everything. I called him an arrogant male chauvinist because he always thought he was right. He thought I drank too much and hated the fact that I smoked cigarettes. But despite the misgivings we both had about each other, we fell in love. After a few years we married, and for many years we were very, very happy together. He was my mentor and friend. We loved the same things. We were both curious about everything. We watched documentaries together and had an intellectual relationship unlike anything I've known before or since.

Meanwhile, my acting career started to take off. I landed featured roles on two series, first "Ryan's Hope" and then the top-rated prime-time show, "Falcon Crest." Mark and I bought a beautiful house in Beverly Hills. We were invited to every A-list Hollywood party in town. I was recognized on the street, asked for autographs, and treated like royalty. Our good friends included the rich and famous, among them O.J. and Nicole Simpson. The money I was earning seemed incredible, the power was seductive, but I would soon learn that the whole thing was a beautiful illusion that could pass with the flick of a writer's pen.

At the time, I blamed cocaine for our problems. Almost everyone in Hollywood in the 1980s was doing cocaine, lots of cocaine. I thought that coke changed Mark's personality. We seemed to fight more frequently. I began to feel that he wasn't there for me emotionally. But when I went outside of the marriage to search for the emotional connection I was missing, I went from having the world on a string to scrambling to survive.

WINTER 1986

Lorenzo Lamas: He Had To Have Me

Have you ever done something that everyone told you was wrong, but you did it anyway? Maybe you were swept away in the moment and made a life-changing decision. Then somewhere down the road you discovered your friends were right—you had been thinking with your heart, ignoring your friends, your family, and your brains. This is what happened to me during the shooting of "Falcon Crest."

I was riding the wave of this prime-time hit television show, which was set in the wine country of Northern California. "Falcon Crest" was created to compete with "Dallas," and we did manage to give J.R. and family a run for the money. On the show I met the son of Fernando Lamas and Arlene Dahl, the hot-blooded, gorgeous Latin lover, Lorenzo Lamas. In the series I played the love interest of Lorenzo Lamas's character. That didn't help the situation.

Lorenzo got very into his role as my lover on "Falcon Crest." Soon he was obsessed with me both on and off the set. He pursued me in every possible way. When I told him I was married, he tried even harder, almost making a career out of tempting me into infidelity.

The fiery and intense Lorenzo perfectly fit the stereotype of a passionate Latin lover. There is no doubt in my mind that he is the most romantic man I've ever met. From the moment he set his sights on me, he filled my dressing room with flowers, balloons, and gifts. I fought his advances until I couldn't fight anymore. One day, in the beautiful wine country of Napa Valley, while filming our show, I finally gave in. I let him sweep me off my feet and fell hopelessly in love.

That clandestine encounter in Northern California made it impossible for me to keep up the appearance of being in love with Mark. My heart and soul were yearning for what surely would be thought of by at least half of the female population of this planet as every woman's dream. Sadly, however, Lorenzo's love for me turned out to be an illusion, a painful, heart-breaking, and expensive illusion.

Lorenzo told me he loved me, that he wanted to be with me, he wanted to marry me. He professed his love over and over again and talked incessantly about wanting to spend the rest of his life with me. I'm sure he meant every single word. Lorenzo does mean exactly what he says, at least at the time he says it. He falls in love, goes completely off the deep end, and loves you intensely with all his heart and soul, fervently, vehemently, unconditionally—until he just doesn't love you anymore. I realize now that he was in love with the illusion of love but, unfortunately, he was the opposite of Mark. He couldn't take the day-to-day reality of a relationship.

During my affair with Lorenzo, Mark continued to fight to keep our marriage together. At one point, while Lorenzo was over visiting me, Mark left a note on Lorenzo's car requesting a meeting. Lorenzo agreed, and they met in a park. During this meeting, Mark begged Lorenzo to leave me alone. He professed his love for me and his desire to keep our marriage together. After the meeting, Lorenzo came over to my house and cried, "How can I leave you alone? You are my life. I want to spend the rest of my life with you."

And so I went ahead with the divorce. I began the wedding plans. I began dreaming of my future with Lorenzo. Life was beautiful, I thought. I was loved by a gorgeous, magnificent, sensuous man. My career was in full swing. And publicity like this, you couldn't buy. We made all the trades, *People* magazine, the television magazine shows. But one day this man who couldn't live without me—who had stolen me from the arms of my stable, devoted husband—dumped me. There was no warning. He simply told me he didn't love me anymore.

My heart was broken, but soon my spirit too would be broken and my career would be at a standstill. Not only did Lorenzo kiss me off one windy day, but because of the weight he pulled professionally at the network, it was rumored he had me written out of the show! And so, with that one brief affair, I went from having a wonderful husband, a home, and a career, to the depths of depression. It took me a full year to recover emotionally and start working to get my career back on track. Though it's pointless to hold any ill will toward Lorenzo after all these years, my heart goes out to other women he, and men like him, have left broken and alone in the wake of their procession of conquests.

BEVERLY HILLS, 1984

Nightmare on Elm Street

*I*f I had it to do over again, I would never have divorced Mark Slotkin for Lorenzo Lamas. But since I can't turn back time, I have to live with that mistake. I feel fortunate however, that Mark and I have remained friends. When we agreed to divorce, he had to address the matter of selling our house. By now the house did not hold pleasant memories for either Mark or me, so the actual unloading of this gorgeous home was a relief for us both. Sometimes I tell people the problem was not with our marriage, it was with the house.

The proud new owners of our home were the Menendez family. They were lovely people. The father was a charming man in the record business. His wife was an attractive blonde woman, and they had two adorable boys named Lyle and Eric. As is sometimes the case, the original builders of a home and the new owners strike up a friendship. Indeed, this is what happened between the Menendez family and Mark. One night shortly after the shocking murder of Mr. and

Mrs. Menendez, I was over at Mark's house cooking dinner. Mark had invited Eric Menendez over. He felt sorry for the boy—somebody had just killed Eric's parents and Mark's paternal side was coming out.

"Eric, I want you to know, if you need somebody to talk to I'm only a phone call away," Mark told him. Mark was a kind person. We were seeing each other again and this poignant moment made me rethink the divorce.

"You're a good friend Mark, I'll remember the offer." Eric seemed pleased that Mark cared. He was polite and obviously came from a family with breeding. In his well-mannered way, he suggested, "Let's see a movie."

We all agreed this would be a good idea. Then Eric spoke up again: "How about the movie *Dad*?" He flashed a wicked smile. "I hear it's pretty good." Mark and I looked at each other simultaneously, without speaking. Like an old married couple, we were thinking the same thought: What a weird thing to say! We merely brushed off the remark and the eerie smile that went with it, thinking this was Eric's way of dealing with the pain of losing his parents.

Of course, within a few months, Eric and his brother Lyle were arrested for shooting their parents to death in the home Mark and I had built on Elm Street. Unfortunately, this would not be the first time I would have a personal connection to a tragic Los Angeles double murder.

Gary Busey: "Scary Abusey"

*A*fter Lorenzo Lamas, I dated a series of wealthy men, many in the entertainment industry. None of the relationships was very satisfying or happy, though there were always some good times. Occasionally I received some expensive gifts from the men, which made the experience a little more memorable. But it wasn't until I met another actor that things got dramatic again.

I've never met an actor who wasn't self-centered. It seems to be the nature of the profession. Maybe what it takes to be successful as an actor is to have an ego that can take all the rejection that actors and actresses constantly receive. Unfortunately, despite other delightful qualities they may have, actors all seem to have one negative thing in common—they expect whoever is in their life to revolve around them and give them their undivided attention. Some actors also have a volatile side, which makes them irrational and very hard to live with.

I'd already gone through my Lorenzo Lamas experience, so you'd have thought I might have learned to keep away from this strange breed of men. But once again, I cast my better sense to the wind when I met Gary Busey, a drummer (he had played with Kris Kristofferson, Willie Nelson and Leon Russell) turned actor. I dated Gary for a few tumultuous months. Gary had an edge, an almost psychotic edge that translated into magic on the screen and mayhem in real life.

And Gary was no different than other actors: the entire world had to revolve around his needs, and those who didn't comply would pay the consequences. I've always had an independent streak—after all, I'm an actress and I've got my own priorities. When I didn't give Gary my full attention however, his response toward me was sometimes very cruel. I endured verbal abuse, rage, and even being thrown out of his home.

I knew Gary had had a terrible motorcycle accident and had almost died. I thought perhaps that contributed to his mood swings. Still, whatever their cause, it soon became impossible to put up with his volatile temperment. Probably what kept me with him longer than I should have stayed was that he knew how to channel his untamed energy into lovemaking. It's been my experience that guys like Gary are astonishing in everything they do because they give a thousand percent. So when they're dancing, they're *dancing!* When they're having sex, they're *having sex!* In bed Gary was tender, attentive, and sexy beyond belief. An insatiable romantic, he would write love letters and even compose songs for me. But the crazy part of him, the raging and the almost psychotic mood swings, were getting more and more difficult to endure.

The final straw came one evening during a romantic interlude when the phone rang. After speaking for a while to his closest male friend, Gary returned to me and began a barrage of questions that were so terrible and abusive that, after enduring his interrogation for what seemed like hours, I felt I had to get out of there just to keep my sanity. Apparently this friend of Gary's, who was quite jealous of our relationship, was determined to get me out of the picture. He told Gary a lot of ridiculous lies. Gary believed his friend rather than me and kept repeating to me after each accusation, "Admit it, admit it!" It was truly bizarre.

Finally I could take no more. Sometimes the passion in a relationship isn't worth the pain. I packed up my things and left.

Gary had a drug problem, I later learned, but I wasn't aware of it at the time. The drugs probably contributed to his erratic mood changes and his abusiveness. But knowing possible reasons for abuse doesn't make being the brunt of it any easier. It's still hard to forget those nightmare days with a very crazy man. To this day, I cringe when I think of the crazed rantings of the man I call Scary Abusey.

BRENTWOOD, 1994

Trail of Tears

My sister, Liza, had been through Hollywood hell. For many years I thought that if I were to get a phone call one day telling me about a tragic death, my sister would be the victim. In the last several years, Liza has worked really hard to pull her life together, and I don't worry as much that I'll get that call.

I never thought the call I would get would be about my close friend, Nicole Brown Simpson.

Nicole and I first met when she was living with O.J. and I was dating my ex-husband, Mark. Mark and O.J. were friends, and Nicole and I soon became friends too. In those days I thought Nicole and O.J. were very much in love, even though both Nicole and I knew O.J.

was never faithful. But there were things that bothered me. I was over at their house on Rockingham one time when Nicole wouldn't come out of the bedroom. O.J. said she had cramps and she didn't want to see anyone. He went ahead and had a good time with his guests. She never mentioned anything about it later. It seemed strange at the time.

For many years we were very close friends. Another friend and I threw a baby shower for Nicole, and when her daughter was born she gave her the same name as the character I played on "Ryan's Hope," Sydney.

Nicole and I drifted apart for several years after I left Mark. But when Nicole decided to leave O.J. the first time, I got a call from her. She said she had missed me and wanted to talk. We met for lunch. She told me about the times O.J. had beaten her. And, she revealed that the time I remember her staying in her room during a party, she hadn't had cramps. She had been badly beaten by O.J. and makeup wouldn't cover it. She told me the fights usually started when she would accuse him of cheating on her. His response was to beat her up, like it was her fault. After hearing about the beatings she suffered, I hated him. I encouraged her to leave him.

I had gotten into real estate to supplement my earnings from my acting career. Nicole wanted me to help her find a place to move to when she left O.J. I found a nice house on Gretna Green, and she thought it was perfect. O.J. didn't want her to have the house and balked at signing the lease. I marched over to Rockingham and told him, "Nicole is entitled to a domain for your children. She should be staying here, and you should be moving out. She's doing you a favor and she's not asking for much.'' He signed the lease, but from then on he really hated me. O.J. doesn't like to be confronted.

After that, Nicole and I became closer and closer. We went running together, had meals together, and hung out. She was focusing on her children and building a life for herself. She seemed to flourish. It was as if a weight was lifted from her shoulders when she was away from O.J.

The last time I spoke to Nicole was the Thursday night before she died. We had talked about going out dancing that night but I was too tired, so we ended up just chatting on the phone. We talked for a long time. She told me she was angry at O.J. over some IRS problem and she said that he was going nuts and was obsessed with her. We talked about men. I was dating a younger guy, a surfer, at the time. We laughed about how uncomplicated the younger ones are, how they just seemed to want to have a good time.

I wish I had seen Nicole that night. It was the last time I would hear her voice.

On the morning of her death I got a phone call from my dear friend, Debbie Chenowith. She said, ''Robin, do you know?''

''What?'' I said.

''I'm so sorry,'' she mumbled.

''Why?'' I didn't have a clue what she was talking about.

''Didn't you hear about Nicole?''

''What about Nicole?''

''She's dead.''

What she said didn't sink in. I must have been in some kind of shock. ''Well, is she all right? What hospital is she in?'' I asked.

"No," she said. "She is dead. She's been killed."

"Are you sure?" I still couldn't believe it.

"Robin," she said firmly, "Nicole was murdered."

"Oh, my God," I blurted out. "He did it."

As the days and weeks went on, I dealt with my grief over the loss of my friend and watched the circus of the century they call a trial. All I could think was, Why couldn't he let her be free? Why couldn't he let her go?

I haven't talked too much about Nicole until now, until this book. Her story fits with the stories in this book because the book is about what happens to women in this town. It is the story of what happens to women in a world where men have so much power and women have so little—Hollywood. It's a book that exposes many famous men in Hollywood who have used and abused the women who came into their lives.

It's about a town where men marry a woman from a good family, someone they can have on their arm at social functions, someone to raise their children. And then those men routinely screw hookers at lunch, have affairs, and joke with the guys about tits and ass. It's a book about a big men's club.

That men's club is a dangerous place for beautiful women. Some lose their spirit and their self-respect by sleeping with too many men for the wrong reason. Others lose their health and their looks from years of drugs and alcohol. And others, like my bright, strong, and kind friend Nicole, lose their lives.

I've been more fortunate than the women in most of the stories told here. I've had painful moments of my own, but perhaps the worst pain I've had came from watching what happened to women I love, in-cluding Nicole and my sister, Liza.

Liza

$\mathcal{L}iza$

HEIGHT:	*5'8"*
HAIR:	*Blonde*
EYES:	*Blue*
WEIGHT:	*125*
PROFESSION:	*Actress, model.*
BORN:	*Colorado Springs, Colorado.*
HOBBIES:	*Dancing, singing, working out, and volleyball.*
EDUCATION:	*Dropped out of Beverly Hills High School.*
FIRST SEXUAL EXPERIENCE:	*Thirteen years old, with a surfer who was seventeen.*
GOALS AND DESIRES:	*To finish high school and become a counselor to help other prostitutes and drug addicts.*
SEXUAL FANTASY:	*To live with a man on an island in the South Seas, like in* Blue Lagoon, *and to have a baby.*
DRUGS:	*Cocaine, Quaaludes, and alcohol.*
HAPPIEST MEMORY:	*When I first got sober and got to know myself.*
WORST EXPERIENCE:	*When I was brought to Paris for the purpose of becoming a sex slave.*
SEX PARTNERS:	*George Harrison, Warren Beatty, Vanna White, Rod Stewart, David Crosby, Jack Wagner, Timothy Hutton, Adnan Khashoggi, Don Henley, and more.*

THE DIARIES

For the Record

*M*y story is not really unique. It happens to beautiful young women in Hollywood every minute of every hour of every day. I was just like most of the other sweet young things who arrive in Hollywood. The only difference for me was that I had some connections because my dad worked in the entertainment industry.

What I'm about to tell you is true. I know, because I lived it. In most cases, I've used the actual names, dates, and places. It is my desire to document my personal life story—what happened to me, how it happened, and why—so that I may help other young girls who have been taken off track by a pimp, a madam, a drug addict, or a dream.

Some people may be upset by this exposé, others may be happy for the publicity, but to me it makes little difference. I'm determined to share those parts of my life that, up until now, I have been hell-bent on hiding. In the folowing reflections, I present to you the Liza I was, the Liza I became, and the Liza I am today.

A HOLLYWOOD CHILDHOOD

How It All Began

I love my parents and I now know they love me, but I wish things had been different when I was growing up. From the time I was twelve until I was sixteen, a relative who lived with us molested me repeatedly. When I told my parents what was going on, they didn't believe me. Had they listened and believed, had I been protected, perhaps some of the things that happened to me later wouldn't have happened. I'm told that many women who get involved in prostitution were sexually abused as children. I certainly was.

Of course, there were other things that contributed to the life I got into: easy access to drugs when I was a kid, lack of discipline from my parents, and the fact that so many men in Hollywood see young girls only as bodies, objects for their pleasure—not as thinking, feeling human beings with hearts, minds, and souls.

I smoked pot, drank, and partied a lot as a young teen. I was a wild child, out of control, and I'm sure I would have been hard to discipline even if my parents had really tried. My mother was a very busy model and my dad's attempts at control were erratic—either he was too into his own life to realize what was going on or he would yell, scream, or threaten me, which only drove me to rebel more fiercely. It didn't help matters that my parents referred to me as the beautiful daughter and to my sister, Robin, as the smart one. Actually, most people think we are both beautiful, and I realize now we both have brains as well.

My dad directed a lot of soft-core porn films and often brought home people he worked with, some of whom I wish I had never met. One time, when I was thirteen, a woman who was an actress in one of his porno films—and I know now, also a prostitute—was over at our house. She invited me to go out with her, and my dad agreed to let me. Instead of going out on the town however, she took me back to her house. A guy was there who gave me four hits of purple micro-dot acid. I had never taken LSD before and this was very potent stuff. As soon as the acid hit me, the two of them tried to rape me. She held me down while he tried to enter me. I started kicking and screaming for them to stop. I was also hallucinating from the acid, and the man's cock looked like a huge snake. I tried to get away from them, but there was nowhere to go. I didn't even know where I was. I went into a corner and crouched in a fetal position, rocking back and forth, crying. At some point during all of this my father called, and while the man held his hand over my mouth to muffle my screams, the woman told my dad that I was tired. She offered to let me stay the night. My dad gave his permission.

I can't recall everything that happened that night because I eventually passed out. The next day, when the woman finally brought me home, I was numb. I couldn't speak to anyone for weeks. I realize now that I was in shock. Unfortunately, I was so shut down that I didn't warn my sister, Robin, about these people. She also went off with the same woman and was attacked by the couple after being given drugs. When Robin and I later talked about what had happened to us, we decided to keep it a secret. I guess we thought our parents would blame us for what happened.

That same year, when I was thirteen, I tried to commit suicide. When I came home an hour late one night, my father went into a rage and beat me. He knocked me into the wall and I almost blacked out. I went upstairs to my room. I felt like I didn't want to live anymore. I had been doing drugs, had been abused by my relative and then by that couple. The beating my father gave me was the final straw—I took out a razor and slit my wrists. As I bled, I wrote "I hate you" all over the walls in blood.

My father came up to my room to apologize for beating me. When he saw me lying in a pool of blood, he freaked out. He got my mother and she rushed me to the hospital. If ever there was a cry for help, my suicide attempt was a loud and clear one. But my parents didn't know what to do with me. My wrists were bandaged and I was kept under observation at the hospital for seventy-two hours. Later I was sent to a different school.

I was not doing very well in school. Part of my problem was that my dad would pull me out of school often to work in his movies. I missed a lot of classes, but I didn't care. I didn't think I had any brains anyway, just a beautiful body—a body that everyone seemed to want.

Robert Evans: Directing the Show

*W*hen I was in high school, I had an older girl-friend named Tiffany. She was almost twenty years my senior but she was still stunning to look at: tall, blonde, legs that never quit, with very, very big breasts. At the time, I loved the company of older women: I trusted them and found their wisdom and lust for life irresistible.

One night Tiffany took me to visit famed producer Bob Evans. I was quite excited. Mr. Evans was a very charismatic and sexy man who had had a stellar career in show business. He had left a successful clothing business at an early age to become an actor. He landed a role in the film *The Sun Also Rises*, and during the filming several stars of the movie—including Ava Gardner, Tyrone Power, Mel Ferrer, and Eddie Albert—had sent producer Darryl Zanuck a telegram requesting that Evans be thrown off the picture.

Zanuck flew from London to the film's location in Mexico to look into the problem firsthand. To the dismay of most of the cast, Darryl Zanuck's decision, spoken through a bullhorn, was, "The kid stays in the picture—and anyone who doesn't like it can quit!" Zanuck's words later became the title of Robert Evans' book, *The Kid Stays In the Picture*. Admiring Zanuck, Robert Evans decided then that he wanted to become a producer.

He went on to produce such notable movies as *The Godfather*, *Love Story*, and *Chinatown*. His close friends comprise a virtual *Who's Who* of Hollywood: Al Pacino, James Caan, Roman Polanski, Jack Nicholson, Francis Ford Coppola, Robert Altman, Warren Beatty, and many more. He wielded as much power as anyone in the business until he was involved in a criminal investigation over a murder and drug scandal that occurred during the filming of *The Cotton Club.*

While being investigated as a possible conspirator to murder, Evans spent many drugged-out days trying to escape the emotional trauma of the investigation and his fall from grace as the most powerful producer in Hollywood. If he was found guilty of involvement in the disappearance and subsequent murder of a financial backer for *The Cotton Club*, he very likely would have been sentenced to many years in jail.

At the time Evans was represented by a man who to this day remains one of his dearest friends: attorney Robert Shapiro, famed for representing O. J. Simpson during the double murder trial of Nicole Brown Simpson and Ron Goldman. Shapiro managed to extract Robert Evans from this messy situation with barely a bruise.

It was during the investigation that I met Bob Evans. In my teenage innocence and my naive trust in my friend Tiffany, I never imagined the purpose for which I was brought to Evans's Beverly Hills mansion.

I've been in many mansions and estates over the years, but to this day I believe Robert Evans's enclave is one of the most beautiful places in the world. Formerly owned by Greta Garbo, the secluded estate is like a palace in an oasis in Tangiers. It is elegant, tasteful, and simply exquisite.

When we arrived, the butler opened the door and

invited us in. He directed us to the living room area directly beyond the foyer. I noticed that everywhere there were huge, round, sienna brown candles that gave off an aroma of vanilla. Beyond the fireplace I could see outside to the pool and an elaborate fountain consisting of hundreds of shooting sprays emanating from the outer rim of the pool, meeting in the center, all lit up by white lights. Beyond the pool was the projection building, a place where private film screenings were enjoyed by Evans' guests.

Music played over hidden speakers throughout the home. Antique furniture and priceless art were complimented by bouquets of fresh flowers. Tiffany seemed unimpressed by it all; she'd been there many times before. I, on the other hand, was drunk with wonder over the abundance of beauty permeating my senses.

I studied a photo of Ali MacGraw, whom I recognized from the movie *Love Story*. I wondered who the man in the picture with her could be. He was stately and disarmingly handsome. Suddenly I looked up, and standing before me was that same man, older, but still striking. He had a deep suntan and wore a white shirt with white pants and white shoes. He smiled an irresistible smile as he slowly undressed me with his beautiful dark eyes.

"Tiffany, who do you have here?" Bob took my hand and kissed it.

"This is my friend, Liza. She's beautiful, isn't she?" Tiffany paused for a moment, waiting for Bob's response. He was too busy looking at me.

She continued, "I knew you would like her, Robert. She's sixteen years old."

Bob's smile got even bigger and his eyes widened.

He turned to a servant and gave him our drink order. He then asked us to follow him out the back door. We walked around the pool and fountain to the large building beyond.

The screening room was like a small movie theater, only more tastefully decorated. As we entered, we saw another beautiful fireplace and those same scented candles flickered on the mantle. To our left was a round table with leather chairs and to the far left a very large, long sofa. Behind the sofa were six huge, custom-designed leather chairs placed against a wall that was punctured with square windows for the projectors. We made ourselves comfortable, and after some small talk, Bob brought out the cocaine.

The three of us spent the next two hours coking up and devouring Quaaludes at a nearly inhuman rate. Bob had pharmaceutical quality Quaaludes, far more potent than the kind you buy on the street.

At some point in the evening's adventures, Bob took Tiffany and me by our hands and led us back around the pool to a patio behind the main house. We made a sharp right turn that took us into his master bedroom suite.

We were all very messed up. Bob seemed so horny at that moment that I believe a lampshade would have looked good to him. As is often the case when men do large amounts of cocaine however, the brain may say yes but the little pocket soldier refuses to stand at attention. Since he couldn't partake in the festivities, Bob resorted to the role he had played a dozen times in the past, that of producer. He began to direct the action with instructions like, "Tiffany, you touch Liza here," and "Liza, you lick Tiffany there." In the middle of our performance, Robert seemed to be struck by a brilliant idea. Asking us to stop, he looked at Tiffany and, eyes half closed, almost too whacked out to know what he was doing, poignantly asked her the following question: "Tiffany, would you please piss on me?"

And so right there, in the middle of this magnificent bed, I watched as Tiffany pissed all over Robert Evans. And I do mean *all over* him. Suddenly I lost it and became very, very ill. I began to heave uncontrollably and couldn't make it to the bathroom in time. I vomited on Bob's newly pissed-on bed and all over his beautiful Afghans. I finally managed to make my way toward the john, while poor Bob trailed along helplessly behind me.

With that, the evening came to an abrupt end. I was so drunk and messed up on drugs that Bob ordered Tiffany to escort me home. I vaguely remember him handing Tiffany a large sum of cash.

On the way home, Tiffany told me that she was a prostitute and that she had been paid for her services for the evening. She also collected a fee for having brought me along. Tiffany made several thousand dollars in cash, but all I had to show for my time was a hangover, some ruined clothes, and one of many early experiences that led to my loss of innocence and the downhill path I later took.

I met Bob Evans one other time. I was dating Allen Finkelstein, and he brought me over to Bob's house. Jack Nicholson was there, and we all watched movies together in the screening room. If Bob recognized me from that earlier night, he never let on. Perhaps he was as embarrassed by it as I was.

My First Trick: For Love

I didn't sleep around much when I was really young. I had been involved with another woman, but after being molested and raped, I didn't usually want to be touched by men. I did feel sexual a lot, however. I would masturbate in my room or in my parents' Jacuzzi. My mom caught me a couple of times and punished me. She made me feel like I was bad, cheap, and dirty. That feeling stayed with me for years. As time went on, I continued to do a lot more things that would perpetuate those feelings about myself.

My first real boyfriend was a guy named Jeff. We were together off and on for a couple of years, starting when I was about eighteen. I really wanted him to love me and thought that if I gave him everything he wanted, he would. He got into trouble stealing some leather goods and told me he needed a thousand dollars to repay the leather company or he would be killed. Naturally, I didn't want anything to happen to him. I knew a girl who had worked as a high-priced call girl. I asked Jeff if he wanted me to try to turn a trick to get the money he needed. I was hurt when he didn't say no, and felt I now had to go through with it. Foolishly, I believed that I had to come through for him or he wouldn't love me.

I went to my friend, who introduced me to her pimps—a couple, Cathy and Al Black. Their clients were mostly wealthy Arabs who paid good money.

When I first met the Blacks, they treated me nicely. They tried to make being a call girl sound glamorous and smart.

"How many times have you slept with a guy for one night and got nothing out of it?" they asked me. "You just feel cheated and betrayed when he doesn't want to see you again. Why not get something out of it?"

Maybe they're right, I thought. Of course, my thinking wasn't the clearest. I was already high on Quaaludes and cocaine, which they gave me as soon as they met me. They promised to send me to Paris with some other girls, where I would have the opportunity to earn five thousand dollars for one night's work.

Before they sent me to Paris, however, they wanted to test me out. They sent me to a client of theirs who was staying at the Westwood Marquis, a very nice hotel near UCLA. I went into the room and talked with the man for a while, but I just couldn't force myself to have sex with him. This guy was really ugly. Why am I doing this? I wondered. I don't want to be here. I told the man it was my first time and I couldn't go through with it. He was understanding and gave me the money anyway.

When I left, Al Black was waiting for me. Instead of being angry, he comforted me and was encouraging. A lot of girls have trouble the first time, he assured me, but he knew I could do it. And he gave me my fifty percent of the money anyway. But it wasn't enough to help solve Jeff's problems, so like a fool, I immediately went out and spent it all on drugs.

The Blacks decided to send me to Paris even though I flunked my first test as a call girl. I told Jeff I had a modeling assignment. I was ashamed to tell him the truth, even though I was doing it for him. I went to Paris with a girl named Diane and about eight others. We were all there to service a single client, whom we were told was a Saudi Arabian king. The first few days we were in Paris we got to shop and enjoy the city. Then the night came for us to see the king. The deal was that everyone would get about two thousand dollars, but if you were picked by the king to have sex with him you would get five thousand. I was more than content to just get my two thousand. That would cover what I needed for Jeff and I wouldn't have to have sex with someone I didn't know. About ten of us paraded into the king's suite that night, dressed to the hilt. He looked us all over and made his decision.

Before I could breathe a sigh of relief that he didn't choose me, I realized that I was going to be part of the party anyway. The king wanted two women. He picked the one he liked best and then she picked me!

I should say here that in order to be a prostitute, you have to be bisexual. A lot of men like a mènage à trois with two women or they like to watch two women having sex with each other. To make it as a call girl, you have to be able to do whatever the client wants. Even though I didn't consider myself a lesbian, I had been with women before and I had told the Blacks about it.

So now, in the hotel in Paris, I was starting to freak out again. I sure as hell didn't want to sleep with this king. He was ugly and fat and old. We followed him into his bedroom. I started to calm down when I realized that he just wanted to watch. It didn't bother me too much to have sex with the other girl. I might have even felt attracted to her, though it was hard to tell what I really felt with all the drugs I had taken to help me get through that night. The other girl and I made love to each other while the king watched. We were both relieved that we didn't have to do anything with him.

The next morning we were paid our five thousand dollars. When I got home, I gave Jeff the money he needed. I then went out and spent the rest of the money on gifts for him. I didn't buy anything for myself. Even though I didn't have to sleep with the king, I still felt ashamed that I had stooped to prostitution. I felt dirty and classless. And I felt I had no one to talk to about what I had done or how I was feeling. It would be years before I consented to sell my body again, but as time went on, I did more and more drugs—anything to dull the pain and shame that were tormenting me. I went out to clubs and got wasted. I partied hearty. And, I got myself invited to the most famous party in town—Hugh Hefner's.

THE PLAYBOY MANSION, SUMMER 1980

Hugh Hefner: Lingerie Optional

*O*ne day I opened my mail and there was an invitation from the Playboy Mansion. Hugh Hefner was inviting me to his annual Midsummer Night's Dream party. It turned out that a guy I had met at a club put me on the Playboy Mansion's invitation list. When I was a little girl, my father had *Playboy* magazines hidden around the house. I'd find them sometimes and look at the beautiful women on those pages. As I grew older, I'd read some of the articles, and once in a while I'd see something about Hugh Hefner. But I never thought the day would come when I would be invited to parties at the Playboy Mansion and actually meet Hefner in person. As it turned out, not only did I meet him, he became a friend and confidant.

I loved going up to the mansion. It's a one-of-a-kind place, even in Hollywood. After driving up the long driveway, past the tennis courts and impeccable grounds, your car is parked by a valet. The house itself is very large and made of stone. The entrance is huge. As you walk in the front door, you are struck by how massive the place is, and how sparsely furnished.

The dining room has a long dinner table where buffets are often put out for the many guests to nosh on. Two staircases lead to the second floor, where there are about seven bedrooms. There is the Red Room, where my friend Marcia and I spent one night when we were too drunk to go home. There are also other rooms referred to simply by their predominant color, the Blue Room or the Green Room. The screening room houses a large screen, video, projectors, and many couches and comfortable chairs. Behind the screening room is a small library.

Outside, beautiful peacocks roamed the grounds. The pool and Jacuzzi are gorgeous. There is an indoor swimming area that looks like a cave—the infamous Grotto—in the center of which is a huge rock. People swim to it and climb on top and sit. Not far from the pool is a sun room, where people who wish to use the tanning machines are welcome to do so.

In the days before Hefner's marriage to his centerfold wife, dozens of beautiful bikini-clad women strolled the grounds of the mansion at all hours. I witnessed many wandering aimlessly down corridors, hoping to catch a glance of Hugh. So many women wanted to be near the Bunnymeister that he literally had his pick of any woman he wanted, any time. Almost all the young women wore provocative clothing and what I called their "just-made-love-to hairdos." Life was easy at the mansion. You didn't have to cook, clean, or pay for anything. Your knockout looks were enough to gain admission to the Playboy Mansion's A-ticket ride.

Some playmates who hung around the mansion in those days, such as Barbi Benton, went on to become successful. Barbi, Hefner's former girlfriend, is now a singer and composer whose music is frequently aired on Los Angeles radio stations. Other playmates have not been so lucky. Gorgeous Dorothy Stratton was killed—her story was made into a feature film. On the verge of stardom, after announcing her plans for a divorce, she was murdered by her jealous husband. She was beautiful and talented, and her death was a real Hollywood tragedy.

Most of the beauties who graced the grounds of the Playboy Mansion during the 1980s reached the peak of their careers just by being there. Making it to the pages of *Playboy* and/or the corridors of the mansion was the highest pinnacle many of them would attain. For those actresses and models who hoped to use Hef as a stepping stone to stardom, the stark reality soon set in. After the mansion, there was often no place else to go. Being a Playmate was not a right of passage to bigger and better things, but the end of the line. Some of the women exploited their beauty to land wealthy husbands, while others struggled along in careers as models, actresses, or singers. But most wound up either hitched to their high school sweethearts or, much worse, drifting into drugs and prostitution. Because my father was in the entertainment industry, I knew that the Playboy scene was just for a kick or two, not for my career. At the time, my relationship with Jeff was not going great, so it felt good to be invited to party with the stars.

The Midsummer Night's Dream party began early in the evening and ended at about five or six o'clock the next morning. The theme of the party was "sleepwear." Famous, infamous, and want-to-be famous people came decked out in pajamas, teddies, panties, camisoles, nightgowns, house robes, corsets—every imaginable type of nightwear. Quite a few partiers had obviously purchased their costume at stores such as Trashy Lingerie, an L.A. boutique whose name says it all.

Hefner didn't like women bringing their boyfriends to his parties. He liked to keep the fantasy going that his girls didn't date, they simply lived for the opportunity to come over to his house and decorate the place. So Jeff stayed home and I attended this party with my friend Marcia, a girl I had met at a club. The men could bring their dates, but more often than not they didn't, preferring to take their chances and see if they got lucky. All the Playmates were there, including the Playmate of the Year. Hef expected them to grace his parties in return for having had the opportunity to appear in the magazine.

Flashbulbs were popping constantly, as people took pictures of everybody half naked and dressed in their boudoir best. A band played music. Butlers poured champagne and passed out hors d'oeuvres. There were rooms full of food and drinks of every kind. Members of famous rock bands, such as Guns and Roses and other rockers du jour, mingled with the crowd. Some people found nooks and crannies in which to act on their lust for each other—there are rooms all over the house where those who were so inclined could consummate their passion. By accidentally opening the wrong door at the wrong time, I interrupted some hot and heavy lovemaking that first night and on many other nights to follow.

When I was hanging out at the mansion, there was an African American bodyguard whose nickname was Scooby. Scooby would videotape some of the guests as they made love. Lots of well-known people were on these tapes, including several of the *Playboy* centerfolds. Hef would often run the tapes on a big screen in his bedroom.

Around the mansion it was considered a high honor to be invited into Hef's bed. One night early in my friendship with him, my girlfriend Marcia and I were invited to come up to his bedroom. We felt honored, like we had been given an audience with Prince Charles. Hef's boudoir was cluttered with books and papers. The furniture consisted of an oversized bed, a huge TV screen, and a video camera to capture all the sexual activities that took place in that room—and to project them onto the big screen while they were occurring. It was more effective than a mirror.

Not long after arriving in the bedroom, Marcia and I were watching ourselves on that TV screen as we performed sexual acts with each other. Hef, a natural voyeur, just watched. He was either too worn out or too old to move around much. We didn't mind. Marcia was very beautiful, and although we never made love with each other except in scenes like this one, we clearly enjoyed it. Even though I had some pangs of guilt about Jeff, I guess I didn't think of this as really a betrayal of him. I probably thought, "When will I have another opportunity to tango in the Rhythm King's bed?" When Hef fell asleep, Marcia and I went downstairs and took a Jacuzzi.

That night we graduated to the "in" crowd. From then on, we were welcome at the mansion any time. I was put on the A list of invitees and became a regular at the mansion for many years.

WESTWOOD, 1980

Betrayals

I guess I thought it was okay for me to play around with a woman, but I couldn't handle the idea of Jeff being with anyone else. He had commented on my going up to the Playboy Mansion with Marcia so often, but he never said he wanted me to stop. Despite my exploits with Marcia and the King of Play, it was Jeff I loved and Jeff I wanted to be with. But one day the relationship abruptly ended. He had a friend whom he hung around with a lot, and I suspected that this guy was gay. I came home one day and found Jeff and his friend in bed together. They were naked. Jeff claimed they hadn't been doing anything, but I didn't believe him.

We had a fight, and I left and went to my parents' house. For the second time in my young life, I tried to kill myself. Fortunately someone found me before I died—I had done a better job slitting my wrists this time than I had when I was thirteen.

After this suicide attempt my parents sent me to a hospital in Florida for therapy and drug rehabilitation. It was terrible. The therapist came on to me, and I ended up leaving after two weeks.

Back at home, I was soon making the rounds of parties and clubs again, meeting new people, taking more drugs. But Jeff was my first big heartbreak—the first of many. I had been willing to sell my body for his love, but apparently even that wasn't enough.

CENTURY CITY, 1981

Bunny for a Day

After my second suicide attempt, Hugh Hefner came to my rescue. He was a great guy in many ways. If he hadn't taken me under his wing then, I don't know what would have happened to me. Hugh arranged for me to become a Playboy Bunny at his Century City Playboy Club.

I was thrilled at the opportunity. What I didn't know was that becoming a Playboy Bunny is more difficult than I had imagined. The official *Playboy Bunny Manual* is filled with more rules and regulations than *The State* v. *O. J. Simpson* jury instructions. Bunnies-to-be are expected to memorize countless pages of text and are then tested on them. And that's just the beginning. The girls spend days just learning how to bend properly. There are numerous ways to stand, sit, and

bend, of course, and the only acceptable Bunny positions are the unnatural ones. For instance, when serving drinks a Bunny is required to arch her back, thrust
her pelvis forward, dip, bend, and freeze. I'm surprised
more girls didn't dive bomb into their customers' rata-
touille. Whoever created these movements had a
strange sense of humor.

After one day of dipping and bending and thrusting
and freezing, I turned in my Bunny ears and cried
"uncle" to Hugh. I wasn't ready for a job yet. It was
too soon after I had slit my wrists and I was on drugs.
Hugh was amused at my reaction to being a bunny
and awfully nice about it. He still let me stay at his
house and took care of me in many ways. The problem
was that he wanted me to be his girlfriend, and I
wasn't interested.

PLAYBOY MANSION, 1981

Shannon Canned

*A*t the time I met gorgeous, sexy, stunning, Shannon Tweed—*Playboy* centerfold and ex-fiancée of
Hugh Hefner—she was falling from the graces of Hef.
But I'm sure the following incident helped Hef decide
to give this beautiful Bunny her hopping papers.

Hugh Hefner wasn't crazy about drugs. They
were the cause of a lot of grief in his life. Back in 1960,
a young, attractive secretary by the name of Bobbie
Arnstein had gone to work at the Playboy Mansion in
Chicago. Hugh Hefner asked her out, they had a brief

fling, and she ended up working as his personal secretary for several years. Bobbie and Hef were very close, almost like family. In those years, the Federal Bureau of Investigation was trying to bring Hugh Hefner down. I guess they thought *Playboy* magazine was too progressive, and—freedom of speech be damned—they plotted to bring Hefner down through Bobbie. She was arrested on trumped-up charges in 1973. Bobbie had traveled to Florida with friends, and the friends had purchased cocaine. Then, back in Chicago, Bobbie was arrested outside the Playboy Mansion. At the trial she was found guilty of conspiracy to sell drugs and was sentenced to fifteen years in jail. Before she was incarcerated, Bobbie quietly checked herself into a seedy downtown Chicago hotel room, left a suicide note, and swallowed pills.

The news of Bobbie's death was devastating to Hef and had a profound impact on his view of drugs. To this day, any reference to drugs in *Playboy* is forbidden, and Hef does not allow drugs to be taken on the mansion grounds. When people are discovered doing so, they are escorted out.

One night, after frolicking on Hugh Hefner's big bed and watching home videos of his previous guests, Marcia and I decided we would take a trip to the sun-tanning room. Hef gave us his blessings and, in his silk pajamas, nodded off to sleep early.

Marcia and I were feeling like we were pretty important people at the time; after all, we had just come from Hef's bedroom.

"Lets get something to eat first," Marcia suggested.

I was pretty drunk and food was the next-to-last thing on my mind—sex being the last.

"Let's wait and eat after we get our suntans," I replied. I was anxious to relax under the lamps. My tan from the summer was fading, and I wanted to renew the fresh, healthy look I had enjoyed a few short weeks ago.

"All right," Marcia was agreeable. She was happy I had introduced her to Hef and would have done anything to please me. We took every shortcut on our way to the tanning room, which was located in a building near the pool. When we finally reached our destination, I opened the door. There was Shannon Tweed with two people neither of us recognized. Like a deer caught in front of automobile headlights at night, Shannon froze. A glass pipe was in her mouth, and one of her friends had a butane lighter—the big kind used to light fireplaces—placed at the pipe opening. He was igniting a freebase high. Shannon removed the pipe from her mouth and in a defensive, angry way said, "What do you want?"

"We came here to use the suntanning machine," I said.

I knew that Shannon Tweed had been very important in Hef's life. To me, though, she was abrasive and rude that night.

"Get the hell out of here. We're using this place now," she snapped.

"What?" Just who did she think she was? I thought. After all, Marcia and I had just finished an "encounter" with Hugh. He had invited us up to his bedroom. And *we* wanted to get a suntan!

"We came here to get a suntan," I snapped back. "Hef said we could."

"I don't care what Hef said. I'm here now and we're busy. So bug off." She turned her attention back to the guy with the lighter, and as he flamed her she went on freebasing, pretending Marcia and I weren't there.

Who did she think she was, Shannon Tweed or something? I turned to Marcia and said, "Let's go to the kitchen where you can eat something."

In the kitchen, we commiserated on how Hef, who had his pick of a truckload of beautiful women, had chosen a main squeeze with the disposition of Leona Helmsley. As Marcia took an apple out of the industrial-sized refrigerator, I noticed a phone on the wall. One of the buttons read: Master Bedroom. I pressed it.

"Hello," Hef was groggy.

"Hef. This is Liza. We just went to the suntanning room and guess who was there?"

"Make it short, dear. I'm sleeping."

"Shannon Tweed."

"That's nice."

"Hef, guess what she was doing? With two guys?"

"What?"

"She was basing! And she wouldn't let us use the suntan machine."

There was a long pause. He finally spoke. "Thanks for calling." He then hung up.

After a few minutes, we heard a commotion coming from the suntanning house. We watched as Shannon and her friends left. We were told later that Hugh had kicked her off the premises. To the best of my knowledge, that was the last time Shannon was welcome at the mansion. Hugh Hefner has a high tolerance for many things, but he won't put up with the blatant use of illegal drugs or with the people who take them. I wish I had learned my lesson about drugs then, but it would be many more years before that happened.

LOS ANGELES, FALL 1981

Rod Stewart: Cheating with the Best

*L*ong before Rod Stewart's ex-wife, Alana, had her own talk show with her ex-husband, George Hamilton, Rod was working up to proposing to yet his third wife, and cheating on them both with me.

It started when my friend Marcia and I—free spirits that we were then—had a threesome with Rod Stewart, whom we had met at a Hollywood party. It was a wild, crazy evening. Marcia and I were getting high on cocaine and Elephant Malt liquor and Rod was eyeing us both, but he hadn't made a decision about which one of us he wanted. Rock stars are known for having one-night stands with any beautiful woman who strikes their fancy. They decide who they want, inform the girl, and the small matter of consent is a given, at least in Rod's crowd. This particular evening Rod simply walked into the bedroom where Marcia and I were lying on a bed and decided to "do" both of us. Without so much as a "Mother, may I?" he smiled that mole-faced smile, took his clothes off, got under the covers at the foot of the bed and worked his way up to the pillows. He was not a shy man.

"Girls, I can't decide which one of you I want. So I'm taking you both."

We didn't mind. By now, Marcia and I had been with more than a few men together, though none of them as famous as Mr. Hot Legs.

After this incident, Rod Stewart chose me over Marcia. The deciding factor? He liked the fact that I had natural breasts! He made fun of Marcia's silicone implants. I really didn't care what his reason was for choosing me, I was just happy about it. Marcia resented me for years, but I didn't care. This was the beginning of an exciting year-long relationship with Rod Stewart that even included the chance to sing backup on his records.

Rod was a wonderful guy in many ways, but in bed, unfortunately, he seemed to suffer from premature ejaculation. At the time I thought that one of the reasons he finished so quickly was that he was worried about his wife, who was waiting for him at home. He would suddenly change from that sexy creature who sang, "If you like my body, and you think I'm sexy, come on sugar, let me know," into someone who should be singing "The Ballad of the Minute Brigade".

We made love in many places—at my mother's house, in my bedroom or hers. We did it at the Record Plant recording studio, on the stairs, on the couch, and at his manager's house. Rod even took me to his own home once. His wife Alana was upstairs sleeping. Our affair lasted until one fateful night when I decided I'd had enough and didn't want to see him again.

LOS ANGELES, FALL 1981

Rod Stewart, "Gift Giver"

Rod wasn't exactly a generous man, except perhaps with his cock. When it came to presents, forget it. That's why I was surprised one day when, after sex, he brightened up and said, "Wait a minute, dear, I want to show you something." I watched as Rod Stewart's little white British buns disappeared into the bathroom. A moment later, he returned carrying a shiny gold box.

Too big to be jewelry, I thought to myself. Maybe it was lingerie. With the excitement of a little boy, Rod began to open the present. My heart quickened with anticipation as I peeked into the box. Rod carefully removed the top and held up a beautiful satin and lace nightgown. He looked into my eyes, waiting for my response.

"Rod, it's beautiful! Thank you for thinking of me."

I reached over to touch the gift. Rod pulled it back toward his famous chest. Without any embarrassment or reservation, he blurted out words I would find hard to forget.

"No! This isn't for you! It's for my girlfriend, Kelly Emberg. I just wanted to show it to you to see if you think she'll like it!"

In a whole year of dating and sneaking around, having sex with Rod on demand, he had never given me a single present, not even an autographed picture. I had given him everything he wanted, anywhere he wanted it, and in every position he could dream up. Now he stood before me, wanting my opinion on a present he had bought for another woman. Where were this man's brains? Oblivious to my feelings, he continued to ramble on about how excited he was to be giving Kelly this gift.

That night, for the first time, I really looked at him. I noticed the wrinkles, the double chin, the pudge in his tummy, that ugly mole on his face. I finally took off my rose-colored glasses. He was actually old and ugly, I thought. And on top of that, astoundingly rude and insensitive.

As Rod rambled on about Kelly, I fought back tears. Silently, I planned never to see him again. He put the gown back in the box and reached over and grabbed me. He actually wanted to have sex again! That was the last thing I wanted. I made some excuse and left.

He called me for months after that. He even rang me up while he was on tour, wanting me to fly out to see him. I'm sure he would have continued having his Liza on the side, even after he divorced Alana and married Rachel Hunter. It was hard for him to give up his little "regular performer," but eventually he got the message. Although I was still letting men use me in relationships, giving them almost anything they wanted in order to win and keep their love, even I had limits. I'd had it with Rod's selfish, inconsiderate ways.

Rod didn't give me the gift I was hoping for, but he did give me a precious present—a lesson in life.

BEVERLY HILLS, 1982

Timothy Hutton Likes to Share

When I look back, I realize how naive I was. I always trusted men. No matter how many times I got burned, back in those days it never occurred to me that a boyfriend would have anything other than my best interest in mind. It took several broken hearts before I finally woke up. Rod Stewart was one. Timothy Hutton was another.

51

Timothy Hutton was the first celebrity I'd ever really dated. Unlike Rod Stewart, I wasn't someone he kept hidden on the side. We went out for a while and I really liked him. He seemed so innocent, so introverted, so sheltered. But sometimes you can't judge a book by its cover.

Timothy took me to the gala premiere of *Ordinary People*, the movie he starred in with Mary Tyler Moore and Donald Sutherland. When we arrived, the cameras started flashing. I was flabbergasted. I had never been to anything so glamorous. There were movie stars, limos, red carpets, and all the rest that goes along with this kind of event. Timothy was a very hot actor at the time but he didn't act like a star. He shyly held my hand and treated me like a lady. He was a perfect gentleman.

Unfortunately, that exotic Hollywood premiere was not a sign of things to come. After that night, we rarely went out. Instead we'd stay at his house, leading the simple life. He was the perfect mate. I was the perfect girlfriend. I did everything right. But maybe I was too nice, because one day he decided to test my love for him. It involved those two things I've had a problem with all my life: drugs and sex.

This particular night, I thought Timothy was going to settle in and read—he was always reading scripts, looking for his next film.

I was surprised when, as we sat in his kitchen, he took out a Quaalude and asked, "Do you want to try a 'lude?"

I thought about it for a second and said, "Sure, okay."

He broke the Quaalude in half and smiled this little-boy smile. In a slightly embarrassed tone of voice he remarked, "Steve will want half of this," he said.

I was surprised. "Oh, is Steve coming over?" I knew Steve pretty well. He was a close friend of Timothy's. Whenever the three of us got together, Steve would act very jealous of me. I never knew if they were more than just friends, but after my experience with Jeff, I knew enough to have suspicions.

"Yeah, Steve will be over. As a matter of fact, he bought the Quaaludes for us."

I wasn't thrilled about Steve's visit. I had hoped to spend time alone with Timothy that evening. In between his usual script reading, I looked forward to making love.

Before long, the Quaalude hit my brain. My fingers went numb and I felt a tingling sensation in my body. I became very relaxed. Quaaludes are like taking a lot of Valium. Euphoria was kicking in, I was drifting.

Timothy then said something to me that shocked me sober. Until then I thought he really liked me, and that we had a special connection. All of that went out the window when he told me what was on his mind.

"Liza, have you ever had a ménage à trois?"

"You mean two girls and a guy?"

He smiled, as if what I had said was a novel thought to him, but quickly responded, "No, two guys and a girl."

I was surprised. I felt weird. "No, I haven't thought about being with two men. And I don't want to either." When it finally hit me what he was talking about, I said, disbelieving, "Are you talking about you, Steve, and me?"

"Yes, exactly."

"But, I'm not interested in Steve, I'm in love with you!"

"Oh Liza, if you really loved me, you'd do it for me. Don't worry, it'll be cool. You're going to love it," he said with a smirk, obviously speaking from experience.

"Do you guys make love with each other?" I wanted him to validate my suspicions.

"We've had scenes together."

What the hell did that mean, I thought? I was getting pretty angry.

"You mean you want me to make love with another man? I thought we had something special."

"We do. It's just that I like to share." He paused, "You want to make me happy, don't you?"

I thought to myself, Liza, there are two ways you can deal with this. You can slap his face and leave, or you can teach him a lesson.

I said, "Okay, fine."

Timothy grinned. Within ten minutes, Steve—the jealous Jezebel, the same guy who had given me looks that could kill because I was with Timothy—arrived with his hard-on in his hand.

Tim immediately told Steve, "She'll do it." Steve smiled.

I felt like a piece of meat. I knew they wanted to use me. Both of them were walking erections. Tim led us into one of the bedrooms. Steve and I sat on the bed as Tim turned to Steve.

"Liza gives incredible head—you've got to try it."

I love giving oral sex. I know Timothy enjoyed my technique because he always used to tell me how good it felt when I did it to him. But just because I do some-

thing well doesn't mean I want to do it with just anyone. And I thought I was in love with this fool!

Suddenly Timothy, the actor, put on his director's
hat and began issuing orders.

"Everybody take your clothes off. I'll be right
back." He headed for the bathroom, but before he
reached the door he turned and smiled. "Don't start
without me," he warned.

Great idea, I thought to myself. On impulse, I decided to do just that, start without him. I watched him
as he took his pants off in a syncopated step, heading
out the door. I didn't think I could feel any more disgusted with Tim than I already did, until I saw toilet
paper hanging from his ass. I pointed it out to him and
we all had a good laugh. As he finally passed the door-
jamb just outside the bedroom, I jumped up and locked
the door. Then I turned to Steve.

"Let's get two things straight," I said. "Number
one, no oral sex. Number two, I don't even like you,
but I'm going to fuck you just to teach Timothy a
lesson."

Before long, there was banging on the door. Timothy was enraged.

"Hey, let me in! What's going on! Open up this
door! Right now! I can't believe you guys!"

While Timothy was pounding on the door, I was
letting Steve pound me into the mattress. He wasn't a
bad lover, but I had no feelings whatsoever for him.
You couldn't tell that, however, by the loud noises I
decided to make just to drive Timothy nuts: "Steve,
you ramrod. You're such a good fuck. Fuck me harder,
baby. Drive me home." I think the final nail was put
in the coffin when I said, "Oh, baby, you should give
Timothy lessons."

When we were finished, I opened the door and said to Timothy, "There, I fucked your friend. Poor baby, do you feel left out? What's wrong? I thought you'd be pleased. Now I've had sex with both of you. Aren't you happy?"

Timothy was so mad that he started punching the walls. I told him I hoped he'd learned a lesson. At the time I felt like I had delivered some kind of justice. But the reality of the situation, of course, was that I was the one who got fucked.

After a year or two, Timothy ended up going out with a friend of mine, Nicolette Sheridan, the beauty from "Knott's Landing." Eventually she dropped him, too. I wonder if he also wanted her to do his friends.

BRENTWOOD, AUGUST 1983

Marcus Allen: Well Endowed

My sister hung out with some of the O.J. Simpson crowd, and one time when I was out with her I met Marcus Allen. He frequented the Daisy on Rodeo Drive in Beverly Hills, the same establishment where O.J. Simpson met Nicole Brown, who was working as a waitress there. O.J., Marcus Allen, and Al Cowlings were all regulars at the Daisy whenever they were in town. When Marcus Allen was signed to the L.A. Raiders, he began to pursue me hotly.

Marcus and O.J. have always been competitive with each other, and I think Marcus wanted a tall, long-legged, beautiful blonde just like the one O.J. was courting. For whatever reason, Marcus was so hot for me, he simply wouldn't leave me alone. He'd make passes when he saw me, ask me out, and call me at home. I wasn't interested. But the worst part was that when I'd turn him down, he'd accuse me of being prejudiced.

"Liza, what's wrong with you? You don't like black men?"

"No, Marcus. I'm just not interested."

"You can be straight with me. What do you have against black men?"

"Nothing, Marcus. I'm just not interested in *you.*"

The truth was, I didn't care what color his skin was, he simply didn't appeal to me. And I resented him bringing race into it. For me, there just wasn't any kind of chemistry.

But when I said no, it only seemed to make Marcus try twice as hard. He was relentless. So I did something I often do to get a guy off my back: I fixed Marcus up with a girlfriend. My friend, Nicolette, liked the idea of dating a football star. And besides, she was beautiful.

It worked. Nikki and Marcus dated for some time. She liked him, and I thought he really liked her. From time to time, the three of us would go out. On one of those occasions, after a night of music and dancing, Marcus invited Nikki and me to come to his condo in Brentwood.

Marcus has good taste. His two-bedroom condominium was decorated beautifully enough to have been in a magazine. We all had something to drink, and after a while Marcus suggested I stay the night so he wouldn't have to drive me home. I agreed.

Marcus directed me to the guest bedroom. He and Nikki disappeared into the master bedroom next door.

As my head hit the pillow, I couldn't help overhearing Nikki and Marcus having sex. It was loud and passionate, and just as I was beginning to wonder how I was going to get any sleep that night, the sounds stopped— they'd only lasted a few minutes. Relieved, I fell asleep.

The next morning, when my bedroom door opened, I expected to see Nikki. Instead I saw this great big, tall figure looming over me. It was Marcus, and he was stark naked! I started to scream, but he held his finger in front of his lips in a shushing gesture. I stopped.

"I'm not here to hurt you," he whispered. I just thought you'd like to take a look at my—"

My eyes moved down to where he was pointing. I was in awe. There before me was the largest appendage I'd ever laid eyes on. It hung down to his knees, and I swear it looked like a redwood tree.

As Marcus stood there smiling and pointing, presenting himself, I took a deep breath.

"What do you think you're doing?'

He continued to smile. He was accustomed to rejection, at least from me.

"Hey, I'm just making an offer." He touched it.

"I'm sorry, Marcus, but number one, you're with my girlfriend. Number two, if I wanted to be with you, I would have done it by now. Number three—" He cut me off.

"It's because I'm black, isn't it?"

I was taken aback, "Marcus, I'm not interested. Now get out of here."

We heard Nikki stir in the next room. Marcus slowly turned toward the door, his penis waiving in the breeze as he left.

Minutes later I could hear them having sex in the other room. Again, it only lasted a couple of minutes.

It wasn't until Marcus dumped Nikki that she and I had a heart-to-heart talk. I told her what had happened. She wasn't very surprised. She went on to tell me that Marcus had a little problem staying erect, at least with her. Apparently the extent of their intimate moments was exactly that—mere moments. She was disappointed in his infidelity, but she didn't really miss him. She'd had better.

PLAYBOY MANSION, SEPTEMBER 1983

Vanna White: The Attraction

I believe there is a little bisexuality in most of us. Some people will admit to this, while others will deny their feelings and be openly hostile to the idea. There have been times in my life when I have preferred a female partner to a male partner. I don't consider myself to be a lesbian, just bisexual. I also believe that women who are truly sensuous can feel attracted to both men and women. I was twenty years old when I met Vanna White of "Wheel of Fortune" fame at the Playboy Mansion. Since it was overflowing with beautiful women then, it was no surprise to find Vanna among the guests; she is the epitome of beauty. Vanna is stunning, but she's also a very sweet person. When we first met, we had an instant attraction. She ignited a passion in me that I had forgotten was there.

Our first encounter included some mild flirtation

but ended when she departed with her boyfriend, an actor who later died in an airplane crash. I went home alone to think about what could have been. I didn't know if my late-night fantasy would ever become a reality. But just a few weeks later, when I was again invited to a party at the Playboy Mansion, I found out.

I was a little high this particular night. I was having a good time mingling with the guests—rock stars, centerfolds, a potpourri of Tinsel Town bigshots. In my peripheral vision I saw a beautiful, blonde, statuesque lady. I recognized Vanna instantly. She was dressed in an elegant gown and was on the arm of her boyfriend. When I glanced her way, she looked up and her eyes caught mine. We stood there and stared across the room at each other. Time froze. It was obvious to me that she hadn't forgotten our brief encounter a few weeks before. I nodded. She smiled back. I felt a flush of schoolgirl infatuation and decided to sashay to another part of the room and flirtatiously look back at her. My tight buns rocked back and forth to the rhythm of the band's bossa nova song. Call it intuition or maybe a psychic premonition—I knew she would follow. And she did.

Vanna whispered in my ear, "Will you come home with me?"

I looked over at her boyfriend and another man who was with them. I didn't know what she had in mind, but whatever it was, I knew I wanted to be with her. I told her I would go anywhere she asked me to. She smiled, and the four of us left through Hef's large iron gates.

When we arrived at Vanna's lovely home, we kicked back and listened to music. Vanna, her boyfriend, his friend, and I made small talk. Maybe it was the music, or the moon, but I knew that somehow Vanna and I would know each other in a very intimate fashion.

Vanna's boyfriend announced that he was going to take his friend home. She seemed to be waiting for this opportunity, and as soon as they left she suggested we retire to her bedroom "to rest."

Her bedroom was beautiful, as I expected it would be. Giggling and laughing, we stripped off our clothes. As soon as our heads hit the pillows, she started kissing me. As tired as I was from the drugs and the alcohol I had consumed that evening, I wasn't too tired for Vanna. She was so exquisite that it was easy for me to shift back into a higher gear.

We kissed each other in a way that only women know how to. Her lips tasted so good. When she touched my breasts I thought I'd explode. I slowly worked my way down to Vanna's flat stomach, and further. Every inch of her tasted like heaven. I drove her wild. By her response, she hadn't felt anything like that for a long time. And when it was my turn—God, she was good.

When Vanna's boyfriend came home, he didn't seem surprised to see us in bed. Vanna suggested he join us, but while I had very much enjoyed the tender moments with Vanna, I wasn't ready for a threesome. They understood. I stroked her long blonde hair and gently kissed her good-bye.

Whenever I turn on "Wheel of Fortune" and smile, my sister doesn't understand. Maybe now she will.

STONE CANYON, JULY 1983

Jerry Buss: Sudsing Up

*S*ome men prefer dating women with youthful, firm bodies. These men will often have a succession of young girls in their lives. And sometimes, no matter how old a man becomes, his age of preference in women remains the same. Of course these men usually have to be wealthy enough to attract young women. This was the case with the multimillionaire owner of the Los Angeles Lakers basketball team, Jerry Buss, who several years ago dated my friend Andrea, who was then very young.

Jerry made his money in real estate and lived every man's dream of owning a professional ball team. He was wealthy enough to collect any kind of toys he wanted and, when he purchased the Lakers, he added one more toy to his collection. According to the saying, "He who dies with the most toys wins," Jerry was well on his way to winning.

Andrea was very beautiful and Jerry seemed to worship the ground she walked on. Jerry, who was richer than most people in Los Angeles, was a superman in Andrea's eyes. Jerry took care of Andrea in every way imaginable: he paid for her luxurious apartment on Wilshire Boulevard, furnished it, bought her clothing, gave her a Datsun 280Z automobile—and he paid for Andrea's mother's apartment and gave her money, as well.

Andrea's mother enjoyed the financial support from Jerry and encouraged her daughter to continue dating him. The word was that when Jerry dated the young ones, it would often turn out to be a family affair. Like O. J. Simpson, he was a generous man and often put brothers, sisters, and other needy relatives through school, as well as setting family members up in businesses. This sports lover always treated his ladies and their families with respect. One evening I participated in his generosity when he took Andrea and me out to a very special dinner.

Jerry Buss had a surprise for that night. He picked us up in his limousine, blindfolded us, and wouldn't tell us where we were going. We drank champagne in the back of the limo and giggled our heads off. Jerry told us our destination was a very exclusive restaurant known for its secrecy and discretion, a place where certain celebrities could safely bring women other than their wives. Jerry respected its sanctity and took the blindfolds off only when we were safely inside. Once the blindfolds were undone, Andrea and I were quickly escorted into the extraordinarily beautiful restaurant. The decor was mostly from the 1940s, very rich burgundy colors and hunter green. Everything about the place was elegant and first-class, like our host. Jerry ordered sumptuous meals of lobster and filet mignon.

The waiters took very good care of us. At one point Jerry whispered to the maitre d', and within moments red roses were brought to our table. It's easy to love a man like this, and for as long as I'd known Andrea she appeared to be in love with Jerry. I was pleased to be along for the ride.

When the meal ended we were escorted back to the limo. We were so high from the wine that we couldn't care less where we were, so there was no need for the blindfolds. Jerry wasn't a big drinker, but Andrea and

I kept each other company, pouring champagne into crystal glasses and continuing to giggle as we cruised up Sunset Boulevard. We were on our way back to Beverly Hills to Pickfair, Jerry's beautiful, historic mansion. As we drove up the driveway we passed at least twenty priceless classic cars. Jerry was a collector of beautiful things, cars being just one area of interest. I looked over at Jerry and Andrea kissing and snuggling. It was obvious to me they were in love.

We entered through a kitchen that looked large enough to service a Las Vegas hotel. It was massive. From the kitchen we walked down a long hallway, passing room after room filled with treasures and tapestries and down-stuffed furniture, not unlike the Hearst Castle in San Simeon, California. We eventually came to a huge stairway. Jerry took Andrea's hand and mine, and the three of us headed up the stairs to the master bedroom. Once inside, it was obvious he only had eyes for Andrea. The two of them disappeared into a sitting room and I decided to explore the grounds.

I headed down the hallway and descended the stairs, counting rooms as I passed. I lost track somewhere after twenty. I headed out the back door and took in the tennis courts, swimming pool, and gardens, then wandered around for a couple of hours. It was easy to get lost on the property.

An adventurous feeling came over me and I decided to take off all of my clothes and dive into the crystal-clear, turquoise pool. Floating on my back, I wondered how many breasts larger than training-bra size this pool had seen. I also wondered what the servants must be thinking, watching my 34Ds from afar as I did my backstroke across the pool, naked. The warm, wet water drenched my body and, floating on a champagne high, I experienced a beautiful sense of relaxation and freedom.

After a while I decided to go back upstairs and check in on Andrea and Jerry. I never expected they would still be making love—after all, he was no teenager. When I walked in on them, they were engaged in a vigorous sex thing. It shocked me at first. But they were so caught up in the moment, they didn't notice me. Jerry was huffing and puffing, and for a moment I worried he'd have a heart attack or something. He suddenly gave out a big heave and released his lip lock on her.

I stepped into the bathroom. Andrea came in a few minutes later. Jerry followed. He didn't seem surprised to see me. A gleam came into his eyes as he suggested, "Why don't you girls have a champagne bubble bath?" We looked at each other, eyes wide with approval. He then called for the butler to bring up a case of champagne. The water filled the tub and Jerry proceeded to empty very expensive bottles of French champagne into the whirlpool tub, one by one. When he finished pouring, he left the two of us alone.

We each eased into the tub, totally naked. We sponged each other off and marveled over the exotic feeling of the thousands of little bubbles against our skin. We soaped each other up, reveling in the luxurious bath. We hoped Jerry wouldn't disturb us—we were having far too much fun.

Eventually we got out of the tub and took turns drying each other off. I was just finishing drying one of Andrea's thighs when I looked up and saw Jerry, the collector of beautiful things, staring at us, mesmerized by our young bodies.

POINT DUME, SUMMER 1983

Matt Lattanzi: Getting Physical in Olivia Newton-John's Bed

*M*y Dad cast me in some of the movies he directed, and he always encouraged me to pursue a career in acting. He believed in my talent and thought I would become a big star. I broke his heart when my career was sidetracked by drugs and, eventually, prostitution.

For several years, though, I did work hard at becoming a successful actress. I took classes, got an agent, and went on auditions. But one acting class in particular proved to be more of a distraction than a help.

"Today we'll be working on improvisation," Vince, my acting coach, told a group of about ten of us in class. He turned to me.

"Liza, step to one side and work on a scene with, let's see—with Matt." My heart stopped. Matt was the most gorgeous man and the most experienced actor in class. He was tall, dark, and handsome and had attained a certain amount of success in feature films. In his role as one of the lovers of Jacqueline Bisset in the movie *Rich and Famous*, Matt was the young buck who pulled down his blue jeans, revealing his perfectly shaped, tight, round ass before making love to her in a New York City hotel suite. It was a sensuous scene. I remember being aroused watching it in the movie theater.

66

Matt and I immediately had a powerful chemistry together. The word was that Matt was an excellent lover, and that his lover and future wife, Olivia Newton-John, had discovered him while filming her monumental flop, *Xanadu*. Matt played the part of Gene Kelly as a younger man. I can only imagine how gifted Matt is as a dancer, and apparently it didn't take him long to cha cha his way into Olivia's sheets. The buzz was that he was a gigolo. Anyway, he took complete control of my heart during our acting scene together.

The next day Matt called my girlfriend, Betsy Russell, who is now married to Vince Van Patten (one of the sons of actor Dick Van Patten). Matt asked Betsy to bring me out to his home. He wasn't married to Olivia at the time, but he was living with her. When Betsy called, I couldn't get dressed fast enough. I was convinced that destiny was taking over. My body was on automatic pilot, ready for take off. I knew I wanted this man.

It was a long drive to Olivia Newton-John's home, along the coast, past the Malibu Colony. When we arrived Matt greeted us warmly and offered us some Dom Pérignon. We made small talk for a few minutes and then he looked me in the eyes and said, in the sexiest voice I had ever heard, "I want to make love to you." I knew this was kismet.

Matt reached out, took my hand, and led me toward the bedroom. I looked over my shoulder at a very perturbed Betsy. Whatever she had in mind for the evening, it wasn't going to happen. Because we came in her car, she was sentenced to a night of listening to our passion as she tried to sleep on a couch in the living room. She could have left me but she didn't, and for that I am grateful.

Matt made me feel like a bride. Compared to other men I had been with, he was so loving and tender. He clearly couldn't take his eyes off of me. As I entered Livy's boudoir (Matt called Olivia "Livy"), I was taken with the beauty of the platform-raised canopy bed. I felt like Cinderella with Prince Charming. We climbed up the steps. He laid me down and then proceeded to make love to me like I'd never been made love to before.

The moon was shining on the ocean, and through the large glass windows moonlight was cascading down on our wet, naked bodies. Matt kept telling me how beautiful I was. As he put baby oil all over my body, he spoke softly, telling me he was in love with me. He savored every inch of my body as he caressed my breasts, my stomach, my thighs, my legs, my toes and back up again. He left no spot untouched or un-loved. He continuously talked about how much he wanted to make love with me, casually mentioning that he hadn't been with anyone but Livy in a long time. According to him, he had been saving himself for me.

He poured baby powder all over the baby oil, mak-ing my body a beautiful, moonlit white. For about an hour, we made passionate love. During the course of this erotic feast he went down on me. I had an orgasm, the first of many that evening.

I usually don't have orgasms when men give me oral sex. For me, it is almost like an invasion of my privacy. The only reason I will allow a man to do this to me is because it makes him feel good. Men think they are pleasing me, but more often than not, they aren't. I'd rather be with a woman. Women know how

to give love. There's a tenderness, a caring, a respon-
siveness that is often lacking from a man.

So when Matt made me feel like no other man had
ever made me feel, and brought me to the height of
sensual pleasure with his lips and tongue, I surrend-
ered to him totally—my heart, my mind, my body.
And that was only the beginning. His penetration took
me to Xanadu and beyond with each stroke. When it
was over, we were both exhausted. I belonged to him
completely.

After a little nap, we went in to check on my pa-
tient girlfriend. Betsy could see we were in love and
needed to be together. She assured us she was fine, so
we went back to the bedroom and made love again.
The most perfect evening in my life ended as we drifted
off to sleep in each others arms—in Livy's bed.

In the passion of the evening and the comforting
dreams that followed, I couldn't have imagined the
nightmare the morning would bring.

"Wake up!" Matt was shaking me. "Come on,
wake up!"

I was groggy. I wanted to sleep. But he relentlessly
jerked me until I woke up.

"You have to go now. Livy will be home soon."

I couldn't believe what I was hearing. My golden
boy was telling me to leave? Was this the same man
who, a few hours ago, had told me he loved me?

"When will I see you again?" I asked, fighting back
the tears in my eyes.

"I don't know. But you've got to get out now. Liv's
on her way from the airport."

I slowly began putting my clothes on. The baby oil
was still on my body. I told him I wanted to take a
shower.

"There isn't time. You have to leave right now."

I finished getting dressed and walked into the living room. It was so hard for me to comprehend that this man, who had said and done everything right the night before, was shoving me out the door. Thank goodness Betsy had spent the night. I don't know what I would have done if she hadn't stayed. Would he have expected me to hitchhike?

The ride home seemed to take forever. Thinking about seeing Matt at the acting class in two days kept me from getting too depressed. I didn't have his phone number. I didn't know how to get in touch with him. The night of the next class, when I thought my heart couldn't sink any lower, I learned that Matt had told Vince he was dropping out. I guess he couldn't handle seeing me—it would make him feel too guilty. I was a basket case over this rejection. Letting go of the promises and the dreams of that night was one of the toughest things I've ever been through.

Matt went on to marry Olivia and have children with her. I saw the two of them together at a restaurant once. Matt couldn't take his eyes off me. Olivia knew something was up; she seemed upset with him, and I wondered if Matt had confessed his infidelity to her.

Olivia stayed with Matt for years, but now that it's over between them, I feel like I can talk about what happened. I eventually got over Matt Lattanzi, but it took a long time. And to my mind, he's still the gold standard in the lovemaking department.

Shep Gordon: Call Backs

I'm proud to say that I never slept with anyone for a part, although many men have tried to get me to. Agents, producers, directors, and casting directors have attempted to date me. They have asked me to dinner or to parties, always with an underlying promise of helping me with my career. My most legitimate roles, however, came from straightforward professionals. I know for a fact that in Hollywood many girls do sleep with men in the industry, hoping to get a part. But I don't believe it works. More often than not, the men don't want to see the woman the next day, much less help her get a part. The poor girls are left disillusioned and feeling used.

Some aspiring actresses don't realize that only a few people can make the ultimate hiring decision. Though casting directors often act as though they can say yes to an actress, in reality they can only present the actress to the director or producer who does the actual hiring. So anyone who goes out with a casting director to get a particular part is pretty much spinning her wheels.

There are many stories about actresses who come to Hollywood, just off the bus from the Midwest, and answer ads in the papers that read, "Wanted: beautiful women to star in full-length feature film. No experience necessary." Sometimes these young innocents find themselves posing nude or even being raped; nearly always they are used and abused. What it comes down to is a matter of young women putting their trust in the wrong people. Sometimes there's no way for these new arrivals to tell the good guys from the bad. My own experiences as an actress have not been too bad, but that's because I know my way around a bit. There is one person I'd like to talk about, however, who had an obsession for me. It turned out to be a mistake—for him.

"The Dukes of Hazard" was a TV show starring John Schneider and Catherine Bach. One of the key draws of the show was the gang of gorgeous babes who ran around in very tight, very skimpy, short shorts and figure-hugging tops. Many of the male viewers apparently watched the show for its tits-and-ass appeal. It's not that I think the show wasn't good, mind you. For its genre—the car-chasing, girl-chasing, police-chasing, general-chasing category of television show—it was one of the most well-written, best directed, well-produced, and beautifully costumed shows. I liked it because there was so much chasing going on that I could answer a phone call during the middle of the show, come back ten minutes later, and not miss much except for a chase or two. It was also a good vehicle for young starlets yearning to break into the business. Most of the time, all they had to know was how to prepare for a good chase—which is exactly what I had to do with Shep Gordon, the casting director on the show.

For my audition for "Dukes," I dressed in tight black short shorts, little black heels, and a tight white T-shirt. I felt particularly confident that day as I walked into the "Dukes" casting office. The receptionist handed me the "sides" (a few pages of script), and an elderly lady checked off my name alongside the name of the agency that sent me. Then she pointed to a room down the hall where I was to wait my turn.

I held my head high, put my shoulders back, stuck out my breasts, and enjoyed the stares from men who walked by on their way to other destinations in the building. I opened the door to the "holding tank" and beheld a startling and unsettling sight: a bevy of beautiful young girls, all reading their dialogue sheets and preparing for their big break. They looked a lot like me.

I took a cursory glance around the room and decided that in order to get this acting job, I had to psyche myself up. I needed to believe I was the prettiest and best qualified. And I needed to convey this to the head ramrod, whoever he might be.

I sat down in a hard metal chair and began to look over my dialogue. Naturally, it involved a chase scene. One of the Dukes was rescuing me from some bank robbers who had taken me hostage. I was required to give a good scream, act scared, and say some forgettable dialogue. Then and there I decided, like a thousand girls before me, that I was *born* to play this part! After all, I was an expert at being chased, profoundly proficient at screaming and very good at showing gratitude to someone who helps me. In the middle of my reverie—just as I was accepting my Emmy for my portrayal of the damsel in distress—I was interrupted by a lady's voice.

"Liza? We're ready for you."

I was led down the hall to a not-so-large office. The woman I was following opened the door and introduced me.

"Mr. Gordon, I'd like to introduce you to Liza." We shook hands.

This was to be the first of many meetings with Shep Gordon, casting director. His eyes widened as he pretended not to be taking in my hard body, though I did catch his eyes drifting downward for a moment, catching a jiggle or two of my breasts as he shook my hand.

Finally, he spoke. "Liza, I want you to come over here, a little closer." I walked over.

"Good, now turn around." I turned around.

"Are you ready to read for me?" he asked.

I began to read, or rather, to scream: "Yyyiiikk-keess! What are you doing?!" The scintillating dialogue went on from there. I must say, I believe I gave the performance of a lifetime. Shep must have thought so too, because he told me he would be calling me back. When he dismissed me, I could feel his eyes on my backside as I walked out of the room. Maybe my mind was playing tricks on me, but I do believe he let out a sigh of approval as the door closed.

For each of the following five callbacks I went to, he told me to wear the same outfit. So I'd innocently trot in and out of his office wearing my little black short shorts, black high heels, and a tight white T-shirt. When he took me over to the set of "The Dukes of Hazard" and didn't introduce me to anyone, I began to suspect that he wasn't serious. During another one of the readings, Shep went on and on about my beautiful legs and how pretty I was. On the fifth callback, as I was going back to Shep's office, the people along the way seemed to be chuckling to themselves as I passed. By now everyone seemed to know me by sight, and they apparently also knew exactly what Shep was up to—everyone, that is, except me.

I was a big joke around the office. Apparently, the

part had been cast a couple of weeks before, but Shep didn't bother to tell me. He just kept calling me back. This fifth callback, he made his move. He asked me for drinks, out to dinner, you name it. He promised everything, but the only job he offered me was the opportunity to date him.

Luckily, I didn't take the bait in my quest to get a part. If he'd had his way, I believe that I'd have been just another notch on his casting couch. I'm glad I had the inherent confidence in my ability to get the job standing up, not lying down. But I wonder how many women before me had succumbed to his callback capers.

I told my father what had happened. He was proud of me for handling the situation the way I did. Angered, he said that these things happen all the time in this industry, but decided to call the producers of "Dukes" and tell them about what happened. It wasn't long after that that Shep Gordon left the show.

L.A. TO PARIS, VALENTINE'S DAY 1983

Imprisonment

*I*t was a moderately cool winter in Southern California. I was pursuing both a modeling and an acting career and had just returned from a modeling assignment at a Beverly Hills boutique. It was Valentine's Day. Modeling was going pretty well, I thought. I had been featured in magazines and was doing runway modeling, and I enjoyed it immensely. I felt so beautiful strolling down the long runway. I liked the feeling of being in complete control of my body. People loved the clothes and they seemed to give me unconditional acceptance, something I'd longed for most of my life.

As I entered the living room my mother greeted me. I was particularly happy because I had been given one of the outfits I modeled that day. I smiled and kissed my mom. She could relate to the natural high I was on, since she herself had spent most of her life modeling. We talked for a moment, and then the phone rang. My mother answered and handed the receiver to me.

"It's for you. He says his name is Michael Bass." I thought for a moment and vaguely remembered that he was the boyfriend of a friend of mine named Pilar, also a model. I had been to his mansion once to visit her. He had said hello for a moment and then he was gone, so I really didn't remember him very well. I took the phone.

"Hello."

"This is Michael Bass, Pilar's friend."

"Oh, yes. How are you?"

"Fine. Great news. How would you like an all-expense-paid trip to Paris?"

"Are you kidding?"

"No. I'm taking some models to Paris to do some shows. One of the girls dropped out and I thought you'd be perfect!"

"You want me to model in *Paris?*" I couldn't believe what I was hearing. I looked over at my mother. She seemed a bit suspicious, but my joy soon overcame her reservations.

I listened as Michael explained that five girls had been chosen to go to Paris on a modeling assignment.

One of them was my good friend, Pilar. He then told me I would make ten thousand dollars for two weeks' work. I was beside myself.

"Is it runway modeling?" I asked him, holding my breath.

"It is," he replied.

I was so excited. Since I didn't have a modeling agent then, I told him he had to get my mother's consent. I handed the phone to my mother.

Thinking the offer sounded too good to be true, she must have asked him thirty questions. I guess he answered all of them correctly because she seemed to be leaning toward letting me go. She looked over at me in a questioning way. I nodded eagerly.

"I guess it will be all right," my mother said, "on one condition. I want to hear from her every day. I want to know how she's doing."

The next day a black stretch limousine picked me up at my family's home. The driver took my bag and opened the door to the sleek symbol of wealth. As I stepped in, I couldn't control my excitement. Modeling in Paris—how divine! I greeted Pilar. We were so caught up in our excitement, it took a few minutes before I noticed the other three girls in the car.

Funny, I thought to myself, these girls are rather unattractive. They don't look like models at all.

Michael Bass was also in the limo. He's really a nerd. More than unattractive, he's actually downright ugly. And he has no personality to speak of. I couldn't understand how he could get someone like Pilar to be his girlfriend.

I tried to make small talk, but none of the girls would communicate with me. They looked sad. The youngest seemed to be about sixteen years old. The other two weren't much older. Usually models are beautiful, skinny, and tall. These girls were anything but. Pilar and I were the only two who actually looked like models. Except for our excitement, the limo could easily have been on its way to a funeral. This was the first moment I had an inkling that something might be wrong, but when we settled into our seats on the plane, I put my uneasy feelings out of my mind.

The airplane ride was great. Michael passed out Quaaludes. We were all drinking champagne and having a great time, and the other girls finally loosened up. We giggled and shared stories. I was beginning to feel closer to them. We talked about modeling, and when the other girls didn't have any modeling stories to share, I passed it off as their inexperience and marveled over the big break they were getting.

Paris was glorious. Even in winter it has a magic of its own. As the limo drove us to our hotel we passed bistros, monuments, restaurants, clothing stores. Then, shortly after checking into the Hilton, Michael took us all shopping!

The youngest girl, Suzie, got to leave her Salvation Army attire behind in one store and walked out wearing a seven-hundred-dollar outfit. We all needed coats, so Michael bought those for us too. We were running around like we had just picked door number two on "The Price Is Right" and won an all-expense paid trip to Paris and a shopping spree. We were in heaven.

Michael told us his company was footing the bill. He wanted us to look good because he would be taking us out a lot. No complaints here—I'd never seen such beautiful clothes in my life. At one point, I told Michael that I wanted to call my mother. He assured me he would take care of it. He walked over to a phone booth and dialed. After a few minutes, he gave the high sign, as though all was well.

When we returned to the hotel, we each had our own room on one floor. Pilar stayed with Michael in his suite, but she visited me often. We'd talk to each other and laugh. We were both so excited to be modeling in Paris.

We had been there two days when it happened. Someone knocked on my door. I opened it slowly. There in front of me stood a tall, thin Arab man, dressed in his native attire. He pushed the door open, smiled and entered the room.

"Michael sent me." He stood there, waiting for me to do something.

"What do you want?" I said.

"You," he answered. "I'm here so you can take care of me."

"What?" I was shocked. I quickly got his point. I thought of the first time I had been to Paris, to "take care of" a Saudi Arabian king.

"I paid a lot of money for you. Now, you take care of me." He sounded menacing.

"I'm not a whore. I'm a model. Get out of here."

"A model?" he laughed. "Call it whatever you wish. Come here."

I didn't move. He started toward me. I backed up to the wall. I was terrified. This man was six feet two, and a lot stronger than me. I looked around the room. My eyes fixed on a lamp. I prepared to grab it. As his hot breath got closer, I started to scream. He grabbed me and put his hand over my mouth. I bit his hand, hard.

"What are you doing?" he yelled. "I paid good money for you!"

I grabbed the lamp and held it up, ready to smash him with it.

"Look, I don't know what Michael told you, but I'm here to model. Now get out of here!"

The man was stunned and, I believe, embarrassed. He left.

Minutes later, Michael stormed into my room. I was shocked—I hadn't realized he had a key.

"Just what do you think you're doing?" he shouted at me. "Why didn't you sleep with that man?"

"What are you talking about? I'm not a prostitute! I didn't come here to sleep with anyone. I'm here to model!" I was as angry as he was.

"Do you really think I'm going to pay you ten thousand dollars to model?" He was yelling. "Are you kidding? What makes you think you're worth ten thousand dollars? You've got to be crazy. You're lucky I even brought you here." I'd heard him talk to Pilar in the same degrading, belittling tone after we arrived, but I never expected him to lay into me the same way.

"You can't do this to me!"

I ran to the door and opened it. Standing in the doorway were two big Arab men. They wouldn't let me out. I was livid.

"Where do you think you're going?" he asked.

"I'm going to call my mother. I'm getting out of here."

Like Dr. Jekyll and Mr. Hyde, the expression on Michael's face changed. He calmed down and looked into my eyes.

"Okay, you don't have to do anything. I'll have the other girls do it. You and Pilar can just hang out and

I'll find some modeling assignments for you. But we'll have to check into another hotel. Pack your things."

I didn't feel I could trust him, but I also couldn't resist the lure of the dream that I so desperately wanted. Maybe he would come through for us with a modeling job, I thought. I didn't want to face going home and telling my friends that I didn't get to model in Paris.

Michael stood there while I hurriedly packed my bag with all the beautiful clothes from the shopping spree. Then he took me back to his room, where he instructed Pilar to pack. He called the other girls and told them to pack as well.

We all met downstairs and a limo was waiting for us at the front of the hotel. We got into it and were driven to another hotel on the Champs-Elysées.

This hotel was small and decrepit, nothing like the Hilton. There was a burly, unkempt man in his fifties behind the desk, smoking a cigar. Michael got two keys from him. Three of the girls were taken to one room and Pilar and I were taken to another. Michael carried our bags to the room and told us he would be back tomorrow to take us to lunch.

The musty room had two narrow beds with one sheet on each, complimented by small, hard pillows. There was no furniture to speak of, just a chair and a television in the corner. Pilar and I looked at each other. She had tears in her eyes. I went to the telephone and grabbed the receiver. I wanted to call my mother to tell her how I was. The man at the desk answered. When I asked for an outside line, he hung up on me.

I decided to go down to the lobby to find a phone. I told Pilar I'd be back, opened the door and walked into the hallway. As I turned to my right I saw one of the bodyguards I had seen at the Hilton. I gasped. I turned to my left, ready to run. There was the other body-guard. Both of them directed me back into the room.

Pilar and I cried.

We woke up the next morning to the sound of a key in the door. Slowly it opened. One of the body-guards put two trays on the floor. Breakfast. Only it wasn't the fresh orange juice, croissants, and flowers served at the Hilton. Our fare consisted of tea and lumpy oatmeal. It was as though we were in prison. We didn't eat.

That afternoon Michael showed up, as promised. He assured us we would be getting us our modeling assignments soon. He told us that we shouldn't be upset about the bodyguards, they were only there to protect us. He gave us Quaaludes again and waited for them to kick in. I told him I had to talk with my mother. He picked up the phone in the hotel room.

"Give me an outside line." Michael dialed a number.

"Hello? I'm calling to let you know that Liza is fine."

I was groggy, but I lunged towards the phone. By the time I got to it, he had hung up.

Once sufficiently drugged, Pilar and I were escorted by Michael to a bistro for a bit to eat. After we finished eating, the Quaaludes were wearing off enough for me to be able to confront him.

"Michael, I want to go home."

He was indignant. "Who the hell do you think you are? We spend all this money on you, take you shop-ping, give you everything, and you think you can just take a plane home without repaying a penny? Not until you earn back what you owe me." He looked over at Pilar. "And you owe me, too!"

Michael must have drugged our drinks, because the rest of the time we spent at the bistro was a vague blur.

The next thing I remember, Pilar and I were walking through the doorway into our room. We weren't feeling well and went to lie down. We were very high, but not so high to have missed the fact that everything was gone—our bags, the clothing Michael had bought on that whirlwind shopping spree, our passports, our money. All we had was the clothing on our back. I went for the door. The bodyguards were still there. Pilar and I looked at each other. We knew we were in deep trouble.

I was scared for myself and particularly for Pilar. She was bulimic and didn't weigh more than ninety pounds. She had been mentally battered by this man and was as weak as anyone I'd ever seen, both physically and emotionally. The phone rang. It was Michael. He wanted Pilar to come to his room.

Pilar didn't come back for hours. I paced the floor. It was dark outside. I looked out the window. We were on the second floor. It must have been about a sixteen-foot drop to the street. A couple of times I yelled out to people walking by, but none of them spoke English. They waved to me, as if I was just saying hello.

Abruptly, the door opened. It was Pilar. I was shocked when I saw her. She was bloody and dazed. She had been badly beaten.

"Pilar, my God, what happened?" One eye was almost shut. Blood was pouring out of her nose. Her arm was bleeding. She could hardly talk. Catching her breath, tears falling into her mouth, she stuttered, "I

. . . there was . . . was an Arab. Michael wanted me to have sex with him.''

"What did you do?''

"I wouldn't.''

"What happened then?''

"They both beat me.''

"Oh, Pilar. What are we going to do?''

"I don't know. The Arab had a suitcase filled with money. It was under the bed, open. I don't think they know I saw it. Liza, he had a gun.''

Terror took over my entire body and mind. I knew I had to do something. Pilar was in no shape to help herself.

I was on automatic pilot; my fight–or–flight response took over. I grabbed the two sheets from both of our beds and tied them together. I tied one end of the sheet to the handle on the window and threw the sheets down toward the street below. I looked over at Pilar. She was a mess. I don't think she realized what I was doing. I went back over to her and held her shoulders.

"Listen. I've got to get help. I promise I'll be back.'' With that I went to the window and, wearing only a bra and panties, praying the sheets would withstand my weight but too terrified to care if they didn't, I made my way down to the street below. The end of the sheet was seven feet off the ground. I jumped. As I landed on my side I heard a crack. My hip and my knee were both injured. Painfully I stood up as best as I could and limped down the street. I wasn't even wearing shoes.

People looked at me as if I were crazy. At that moment, I probably was. I remembered having seen a disco about a block away. I ran into the disco and begged for help. The manager—thank God—spoke English. He gave me a coat to wear and took me in the back. He let me use his telephone, and I called an attorney friend of mine in the United States, collect.

For the next two hours I waited while my friend called the FBI and the FBI called Michael Bass. My friend finally called me back.

"Listen, Liza," he said. "The FBI has called him and told him that if he doesn't return your clothes and passport and put you and Pilar on the morning plane to Los Angeles, he will be facing serious charges."

"What should I do?"

"Go back to the hotel, but have someone accompany you."

"Are you sure it's safe to go back?" Terrified, I remembered the gun Pilar had seen.

"Yes. This guy knows he's in trouble if he doesn't do as he was told by the FBI."

After thanking my friend, I told the disco manager what had happened. Fortunately, he agreed to accompany me back to the hotel. When dawn came, we both went back to meet with Michael.

Pilar was curled up in a ball on the bed. My friend was right, Michael was going to cooperate. As a matter of fact, he insisted on traveling back with us.

I thought about the other girls. After checking into the second hotel and saying good-bye, we never saw them again.

During the entire flight, Michael apologized and begged me not to press criminal charges. But the moment I got off the plane I went straight to the FBI.

The FBI was excited to have me as a witness. They had been after this guy for a long time. But to this day, they haven't been able to bring charges against him.

Pilar backed out of testifying. My lawyer tried to convince me that it was futile to go after Michael. He said that Michael's lawyer would try to make me look bad, make it seem like I was a prostitute, which would have been devastating for my modeling career. When he finally refused to help me and insisted I drop the case, I figured he took the $50,000 Michael had offered me not to testify.

Michael Bass never paid for what he did to me, what he did to my friend or to the other young women who disappeared. As far as I know, he is still in the business of brokering young girls—telling them they will be going to Europe on modeling assignments, then turning them into white sex slaves.

I feel compelled to put my life on the line to write about him. If I wasn't successful in getting a court of law to put him away for his crimes, at the very least I can warn other young girls so that they won't fall prey to this sex-slave con game or others like it.

Sometimes I think about those three lonely souls in that limousine on that cold day in February. I wonder if they ever made it home.

LAS VEGAS, SPRING 1984

Adnan Khashoggi: Ten Thousand Dollars for One Hour of Sex

I returned from a trip to New York with my sister and couldn't stop talking about a man we both had met by the name of Victor. He was a very attractive, well-groomed, and exceedingly charming man. I guess I had a crush on him, even though he was married. Victor told me that he worked for one of the richest men in the world, Adnan Khashoggi. I would soon learn what Victor did for Mr. Khashoggi, but I didn't know at the time.

A short while later, I received a phone call from Victor inviting me to Las Vegas for a week. He said he wanted me to meet his friends and his boss. He promised it would be fun and said not to worry about the expenses—his boss would take care of them. I was excited.

The next day a limousine picked me up and took me to the airport. It was the first time I flew first class. The service was wonderful. I didn't want the flight to end. When I stepped off the plane in Las Vegas, a chauffeur was waiting for me. He was holding up a card that read LIZA/KHASHOGGI. He led me to the waiting stretch limousine while another bodyguard picked up my luggage. I was escorted to the limo. People were looking at me as if I were someone important. For the first time in my life, I really felt that I was. I had been to Las Vegas before, but I always carried my own bags. This was wonderful. I knew what it must feel like to be royalty.

We arrived at the hotel. Adnan Khashoggi had an entire floor for himself, his bodyguards, and his entourage. I was led to my own suite. I gasped when I entered the room. The ceiling was fifteen feet high, the drapes were velvet, the furniture exquisite. Fine crystal and china everywhere graced the tables. It was unlike anything I had ever seen. I was told to make myself comfortable and to prepare myself for the evening.

The first thing I did was take a long, luxurious bubble bath. The huge marble Jacuzzi tub was too inviting to resist. I wasn't sure of what lay ahead, but I was content to be exactly where I was.

As I toweled myself off, I looked in the mirror and admired my perfect, youthful body. From comparing myself with the other girls in my high school gym class, I knew my figure was above average. I was a tall, natural blonde, with firm breasts, a tiny waist, slender hips, and long, muscular legs. I wondered if Victor would be seeing me this way soon, and what his reaction would be. I heard a knock at the door. It must be Victor, I thought.

I didn't bother to dress. I thought it would be far more seductive to simply wrap a towel around my just shampooed hair and a second towel around my torso, tucked neatly above my breasts. I opened the door, expecting Victor. He was there, but standing next to him was a short, stocky man wearing a button-down collar shirt. To look at him, you would never guess that he was one of the most influential and wealthiest men in the world. The little wisps of hair on the top of his head were neatly in place. There was something self-effacing about him, like a kid who was about to open a present he wasn't quite sure he deserved. Adnan was very sweet and respectful as Victor introduced him to me.

"Liza, I'd like you to meet Adnan." Victor smiled, quite pleased with himself.

"Hello. Nice to meet you." We shook hands.

After some small talk, Adnan gave me an envelope and said, "Here is ten thousand dollars."

Surprised, I said, "Why are you giving me money? I have my own money on me."

Victor interjected, "Just take the money. He wants you to go and buy a nice dress."

By this time, I had been around enough to know what was going on. I turned to Victor, angry and disappointed, and said, "I'm not a prostitute. I don't want the money."

Adnan smiled at me, amused, and said, "Come and see me when you are dressed." Then he tossed the money on the floor and walked away with Victor. After he was gone, I scooped the money up and counted it. It was ten thousand, all right.

Victor called a few minutes later and asked me to cooperate. "He has a crush on you. Just have dinner with him. You don't have to do anything if you don't want to."

When I hung up, I called a friend in L.A. who did secretarial work for one of the better known madams, Madam Alex. My friend told me that from everything she had heard, Khashoggi treated his girls pretty well. She advised me to take advantage of the situation. In retrospect I wish she had given different advice, but at the time I thought, fuck it. What do I have? Nothing. I might as well go along with this.

I got dressed and went over to Khashoggi's suite. We talked for a while and he seemed really nice. In fact, he was one of the nicest, most generous "johns" I would ever meet. He handed me a bottle of blues—pharmaceutical Quaaludes—and a two-gram bottle of coke. He told me to go buy a dress and meet him for dinner.

When I left him, I took three of the Quaaludes and went shopping. I bought a gown and several pairs of shoes. Then I went back to my room and passed out. The Quaaludes were much stronger than I had realized they'd be. Dinnertime came and went. Adnan's people pounded on the door, but I was out cold. Finally, Victor came in. He roused me a little. I was groggy. I guess he thought that raping me would wake me up. He pulled down his pants and tried to fuck me. I resisted as well as I could. He tried to get me to give him head, but in the drugged-out state I was in, that didn't work. Finally he gave me some coke, hoping it would wake me up. He told me I had no choice but to "do" Adnan now because I had spent his money. Furious, though my anger was somewhat numbed by the drugs, I said, "Why did you set me up? I'm not a fucking prostitute!" I don't know how he replied, but I know I hated him. He was a fucking pimp who had completely betrayed me and used me. He even betrayed his boss by trying to rape me. And he certainly didn't give a damn what happened to me.

Finally I pulled it together enough to walk, and a bodyguard brought me to Adnan's suite. He soon led me into his bedroom and the next thing I knew, he lifted the caftan he was wearing, exposing his erection. Even as sedated as I was, I knew what was expected of me. And it was one thing I did well—I had been in training for many years. I serviced him. He seemed very satisfied. When it was over, he directed me to the bathroom.

"Now, go take a bath. I want you clean." Then he added. "When you are finished with your bath, look under your pillow."

I went to the bathtub, poured in some lavendar bubble bath, and climbed in. I was angry, disgusted, and humiliated. I wanted to be clean, too, but it would take more than a bath to restore me.

After the bath I came out and looked under the pillow. I picked up a matching bracelet, earrings, and ring, all glittering with exquisite diamonds, rubies, and sapphires.

The next day I left the hotel without telling anyone. Victor called me when I got home and asked what happened to me. He said Adnan had wanted to say goodbye. He liked me and wanted me to fly to Geneva to stay with him. Victor sent me the ticket, but I cashed it out. That was the last I saw of Adnan Khashoggi and his pimp, Victor. Khashoggi admittedly was a very generous man. But the high price he pays, the expensive gifts he gives, the royal treatment his women receive, seduce all too many young, beautiful girls into becoming hookers. Innocently and foolishly, they believe every trick will be as profitable and relatively painless as Khashoggi. I know because that is what happened to me. Khashoggi, my second trick, may have been the most glamorous, but all it did was lead me further down the path of self-hate, shame, and self-destruction. In the years to follow, when I wasn't dating a man who could supply me with drugs, when I needed money to support my growing habit, I would turn to prostitution again and again.

BEVERLY HILLS, 1985

George Santo Pietro: Hot Coffee Enemas

*L*ong before he could boast of being the husband of Vanna White, George Santo Pietro owner of Santo Pietro restaurant, was with me. He was an older man, forty-seven, and at the time I was barely out of my teens. We lived together for two years.

George had been seeing actress Linda Evans before he began dating me. He was rich and, at first, like a father figure to me. He bought me anything I wanted, including a car and lots of clothes. We lived in the same neighborhood as Don Henley and Warren Beatty. The house we shared was beautiful. It had a long, steep driveway, a guest house, a pool, a sun deck, and lots of glass windows offering beautiful views. Behind our master bedroom was a huge steam room and bathroom with lots of mirrors.

I was crazy about George, but even though he said he wanted to have a baby with me, he couldn't seem to keep his dick in his pants. I didn't know it at the time, but while we were living together he was still seeing Linda Evans. As a matter of fact, he was so low in the fidelity department that he even tried to fuck my sister.

Another thing this Italian rogue had going for him was that he was a good lover, one of the best I had had at that point in my life. He was virile and had a great body and—usually—I loved being with him. There was, however, one particular kinky thing he did in bed that makes me shudder to this day. At the time I was so in love, I would have done anything to please him. And I did.

Often, before we had sex, he'd lead me into his steam room. He would fill an enema with coffee and hot water. He'd then put it up my butt while we did "sixty nine"—he licked my pussy and I sucked on his cock. All the while, he had this hot coffee enema shoved up my ass. When the pain got too excruciating to describe, I begged him to let me go to the bathroom, but he wouldn't let me—not until he climaxed.

The first time George did this to me, I was so caught up in loving him that I tried to think of it as interesting. But when he did it a second time, I admitted to myself that it was really unbearable. I told George that I didn't like the ordeal at all. I think that turned him on even more because he insisted on doing it. The more fervently I protested, the more frequently he subjected me to this torture.

Unbelievably enough, it wasn't these hot-coffee enemas that finally drove us apart. George Santo Pietro was someone I thought I loved and whom I thought loved me, so I hung in there. I put up with verbal and physical abuse as well as this perverse and sadistic sexplay. I had too little respect for myself at the time, and I wanted love too desperately. We only broke up when I finally realized that he had been cheating on me during the whole relationship.

Looking back, those painful sexual encounters were something I wish had never lived through. I cringe in horror when I think of how many sweet young women this man may have forced his sadistic ways upon, including Vanna White.

BIRTHDAY, 1986

George Santo Pietro: Knife Wielding

*D*uring the height of our affair, George Santo Pietro threw a birthday party for me that haunts me to this day. It began innocently enough, with an American Express card.

"Here's my credit card. Buy any dress you want for your birthday party," he said.

I knew just where I wanted to buy my dress: Charles Gallay Fashions on Rodeo Drive in Beverly Hills. The saleslady helped me pick out a beautiful eight-hundred dollar number. I felt simply elegant. When the evening of my party came, I couldn't wait to show George my new dress.

As I stood in front of the bathroom mirror, I sighed. I looked beautiful. Tonight was my night. Over a hundred people would soon be arriving to help me celebrate my birthday. When I finished putting on my earrings, I adjusted the thin strap on my gown and took a deep breath. I hadn't shown George my dress yet and couldn't wait to surprise him. I searched through the house, passing butlers and caterers who all expressed approval at how I looked. I finally found George in the kitchen, tasting the evening's fare. He looked at me critically.

"What the hell have you got on?" he demanded.

"The dress I bought. Remember, you told me to buy a dress?"

"You look like a whore! It's too late to return it.

94

The guests will be arriving any minute. Don't you have any brains?''

I felt humiliated. I felt stupid. I felt terrible. Just then the doorbell rang.

"Go answer it, bitch." He often talked to me like this. I walked to the front door, holding back tears.

The first to arrive was my girlfriend, Julie. "Liza, you look divine." Julie could tell I was upset. "Let's go to the bathroom, Liza. I have a treat for you." She gave me some Quaaludes to help me relax. We both had a drink, and I went about the business of being the charming hostess. In between my greetings, compliments, and birthday wishes, I had a few more drinks.

Everybody was there—Warren Beatty and a dozen other movie stars. I noticed a friend, Mitch Gaylord, who had won a gold medal at the Olympics in gymnastics. What a hunk. He was staring at me from across the room. I flirted. He approached. We talked.

"So, you're the birthday girl," he said. "Happy birthday, Liza."

We continued to talk and flirt. Out of the corner of my eye I could see George watching me. He looked over from time to time, and although he smiled, I knew he wasn't pleased.

"Show me what you can do, Mitch!" I said flippantly, not expecting he actually would. Before I could say I was just kidding, Mitch Gaylord was putting on a show for me right there in the living room.

Mitch gave new meaning to the term hard body. The man was a dream. He proceeded to do flips, six of them in a row. Then he did a triple flip into the air and landed perfectly. Wow! What a turn on! When the music started, Mitch and I began to dance. I was having something I hadn't had in a long time: fun. After a while, my girlfriend Julie cut in. Mitch looked surprised, but he gave me up without a fight. Julie and I danced sensuously, like Madonna and Sandra Bernhard. When the slow songs came on, we danced slowly and passionately, looking into each other's eyes with love. Julie was the first girl I had been with and we had always been close, ever since our first kiss back in high school. Julie seductively ran her hand up and down my back, going lower with every caress. I sensed someone looking at us, giving me the evil eye. Suddenly my worst fear became a reality. George, smiling, grabbed me by the arm. He said he had a surprise for me and took me downstairs. Here, when we were alone, he leaned me up against a freezer. He began to caress my cheek and stroke my hair.

"Liza, I have a present for you."

I thought the dress had been my present. Curious and excited, I said, "What is it?"

He pressed hard against my neck with one hand. Behind his back, his other hand gripped the surprise—a huge kitchen knife. He held the knife in front of me in a threatening way and hissed, "You're embarrassing me and treating me with disrespect. You better not do this again."

I was afraid he was going to kill me. Even the drugs couldn't deaden the terror.

"I'm sorry," I tried to calm him down. "It's just that it's my birthday. I'm having a good time."

He was obviously jealous about Julie and Mitch Gaylord. The next two minutes seemed like an eternity. He shoved the knife into my neck, nearly breaking through the skin. I froze in fear. I was afraid to scream or to move. Finally, he let me go.

We both walked back upstairs. For the rest of the night, I ignored Mitch Gaylord and Julie Smith. Julie seemed to understand, but I'm not sure Mitch knew what was going on.

By the end of the evening, George had put the move on another girlfriend of mine. I saw him kissing her in the kitchen. My sister Robin told me that he even hit on her that night! And Warren Beatty was hitting on me, as he had so many times before—probably trying to collect on his bet with George on whether or not he could get me into bed.

It was a birthday to remember.

BEVERLY HILLS, WINTER 1987

Warren Beatty: Nothing to Write Home About

When I lived with George Santo Pietro, our next door neighbor, Warren Beatty, would visit often. When George was out of earshot, Warren would inevitably start telling me how beautiful I was and how much he needed to make love with me.

All the gossip about Warren Beatty and his obsession with women is true. He seems to go after just about every good-looking woman he meets. To my mind, it's a personality flaw or a sex hormone problem, though some may think of it as an enviable trait. His reputation for needing ''new meat'' is about as renowned as his sister Shirley MacLaine's reputation for not needing it—her spiritual orientation apparently takes care of her baser human desires. No matter.

Warren has enough sex drive for the two of them. The women Warren hasn't spent time with, believe me, he didn't want. But for the woman Warren is attracted to, he doesn't stop his relentless pursuit until he has bagged his prey.

Just like his character in *Shampoo*, Warren doesn't care if the lady is attached, unattached, interested, not interested, what she thinks or where she's coming from. As a matter of fact, the only real prerequisite for Warren to zero in on a female and make her the object of his pursuit is that she be young and beautiful. When I lived next door, George and I watched sexy, hard bodies parade in and out of his home, one after the other. It was the talk of the town.

One night during my stint with George, I caught him in a lie. He had been out most of the evening. When he came in, he had lipstick on his shirt and he smelled like a particular part of a woman's anatomy. The next day I was still nursing the wound I received from the smack he'd given me when I questioned him.

I'd suspected George was still seeing Linda Evans—she'd call, he'd leave the house, the usual. And now this. I'd been thinking about how to get back at George for a long time. There are very few ways a woman can get back at a man, but sleeping with his best friend is one. And although the idea of being with another man repulsed me, especially someone as old and out of shape as Warren, I made the decision to go ahead and do it.

I called Warren on the phone and told him I'd changed my mind. He knew what I meant. "Come over right away, Liza. I'm waiting for you." What I didn't know at the time was that he had company—Sean Penn, Madonna's ex.

I put on a beautiful outfit, sans underwear, and walked next door. I rang the bell on the iron gate. The maid spoke through the call box and buzzed me in. I walked up the driveway and the maid was waiting for me at the large front door. She led me back into the living room, where I was surprised to see Warren and Sean sitting, both smiling. To this day, I don't know if Warren had thoughts about a threesome, but I wasn't interested. It's one thing to get your boyfriend jealous by making love with his friend. It's quite another to become the whore of the neighborhood. Neither George nor Warren knew about my past experiences, and I wanted to keep it that way. I made small talk for a few minutes and told my hosts I had to go. After that night, Warren's relentless pursuit escalated to the point where he simply would not leave me alone. He actually began to beg.

Warren told me he couldn't sleep at night; thoughts of me took over. His lust for me was driving him mad. He had a hard time concentrating on a movie project he was doing. He said he never wanted anyone as badly as he wanted me. He even talked about love. He said he really thought he was in love with me.

Meanwhile, George continued to treat me badly. Besides the verbal and physical abuse and the sadistic sex, it was obvious to me that there was at least one other woman in his life. So, I finally agreed to meet Warren, partly for revenge against George, but also out of pity for Warren. The poor man had told me he simply couldn't function without me. I'd been there myself, I knew what unrequited obsessive love felt like. I decided to have sex with him that afternoon, at my mother's house near Beverly Hills.

Mom was expected home soon, so the pressure was on. I figured I'd greet Warren, we'd make small talk, have a Pepsi, and then head up to one of the many bedrooms upstairs. Even if my mom came home, she wouldn't know I was there, who I was with, or what we were doing. The doorbell rang. I looked in the mirror. My hair looked good, my makeup, my dress—I was ready. And who knows, I thought, maybe there could be something between us. After all, he was in love with me and I was, for all practical purposes, available. Maybe we could start a relationship. I wouldn't have far to move my things. I'd get him on a good exercise program and get rid of all that flab, and perhaps find him a good plastic surgeon to take up the slack on the skin left over. As I slowly opened the door, still lost in my reverie—*bam*. I felt like my body had been hit by a truck. I was being shoved across the room.

The wind had been knocked out of me and it took me a moment to get my bearings. I quickly realized that Warren Beatty had pushed me back and shoved me down onto a couch. He was all over me. Breathing hard, hands groping, he was an animal. I could feel one of his hands in my panties, his fingers roughly grabbing at me. He was hurting me. The other hand was ripping off my clothes. His legs were entangled with mine. Without so much as a "how dee do," his close to two-hundred-pound frame was squashing the breath out of my body. The next minute or so is a blur, but within that time he had an orgasm. It was over as quickly as it had begun. Without a word, he put his pants and shirt back on, then combed his hair in the mirror—the same mirror I had only minutes earlier been gazing in to, dreaming about the possibilities. He then opened the door and left, never to be seen again.

Thinking about it now, I know I was naive to think that Warren had actually fallen in love with me. While it isn't news to many women that some men will say and do anything to get a woman in bed, for me it was another tough lesson. I really believed Warren felt something for me. He's a pretty good actor, after all. Whatever he might have felt, it didn't include caring enough to make a phone call once he'd had his way.

Shortly after Warren Beatty won his bet and got into my panties, I broke up with George and went to live back at home with my mom. Some time later, George Santo Pietro married Vanna White.

And so it goes, in Hollywod.

CIRCUS, CIRCUS, SPRING 1987

Don Henley: Ringside Entertainment

I had met rock star Don Henley, then with the Eagles, through George Santo Pietro. After George and I broke up, I went out with Don for a while. He is one of the worst cocaine addicts I have ever seen. I liked hanging out and sometimes sitting at a piano and singing with him, but I hated how he smelled. It wasn't that he didn't bathe, it was just that he had done so many drugs and had drunk so much alcohol in his life that the smell came out through his skin.

Early one night, after we had been dating for a while, my sister dropped me off at his recording studio. When he saw me, he said, "Liza, I have a big surprise for you."

"What?" I asked. I was pretty excited.

"I'm not going to tell you. I want to show you."

We went back to his house, did some lines of coke, and he gave me a gold Cartier watch with diamonds on it. It was beautiful. I thanked him, but he quickly told me that that was not the surprise. What has gotten into him, I thought.

"Let's go shopping," he said.

I jumped in the car with him, anticipating that we were headed to Neiman Marcus or Saks. Unfortunately, we ended up at Circus Circus, the popular sex store.

I'm not a big believer in sex toys, dildos and the like, but Circus Circus has it all. Their shelves were stocked with everything you can think of: chains, whips, videos, magazines, toys, games, lotions, potions, paddles, shackles, handcuffs and pussy puffs. Wandering around the store, I wondered what Michelangelo had designed those perfectly shaped penises, complete with natural curves and veins. Even more importantly, who posed for them? I had to laugh when I saw blow-up dolls with permanently open mouths and orifices, shaped into perfect Os, inviting heaven knows what to be inserted into each expandable opening. I guess for some horny people anything will do. The upside, I suppose, is that they don't have to take their date out to dinner or remember her birthday—or for that matter, her name.

To me, it was a big joke. But Don was like a kid in a candy store. By the time we left, he had picked out a vast array of erotica, including dildos and massage oils in several flavors.

It was not ten minutes after we arrived back at Don's home that the doorbell rang. Don ran to answer. When the door opened, five girls came in, all young, all prostitutes. I knew two of them. Don said to me,

"This is your surprise!"

He immediately started an orgy with these women, and I was left to watch. I began to wonder why I was there at all, until he said, "Liza, go get the bag of toys we just bought."

When I came back, I saw that one of the women was having a hard time with the whole scene. Don and the other girls were just ignoring her. By now I was feeling that I, too, had had enough of Don's surprise. He was paying these prostitutes a thousand dollars each, and he expected me to join the party for free. I approached the girl who looked freaked out and said, "Let's get the fuck out of here."

That night, she told me this was her first prostitution job. She was a drug addict and she needed the money for drugs. I told her to get out of prostitution. She'd really regret it. I later found out that she took my advice. That was the one good thing that came out of my experience with Don Henley: I helped convince one woman not to sell her body.

Despite repeated phone calls in the following weeks for me to go out with him again, I decided Don Henley was a mind fuck I could do without.

HOLLYWOOD HILLS, OCTOBER 1987

Jack Wagner: Personally Signed Autograph

The Screen Actors Guild has 78,000 members nationwide, and most of these actors and actresses are out of work. Given that fact, I don't understand how, when an actor hits, he can forget about the time he was an unknown in a sea of competition.

Several years ago my friend Cheryl Bergoff, who has since married actor Rob Lowe, introduced me to Jack Wagner. At the time, Jack was an actor on "General Hospital." Now he's on "Melrose Place." Anyone who knows who he is will tell you he's absolutely gorgeous, the drop-dead-in-your-tracks kind. We were introduced at a Halloween party and hit it off immediately.

By the end of the evening however, he acted like he never wanted to see me again. I would have felt hurt, but earlier Cheryl had told me the rumors about his sexual orientation—it seemed he wasn't only attracted to women. So I chalked it up to a bewitching evening of entertainment and said, "Adiós."

The next time I saw Jack, some weeks later at a restaurant, he kept looking at me. Eventually he came over to my table. He told me how gorgeous I was and asked me out on a date. At first I was apprehensive. Then I figured that maybe he was on the fence about his sexual orientation, and I ought to help with his decision.

Jack picked me up at my home. From the moment he arrived, he seemed to be excited to be there. It was obvious he was pleased with my appearance—I wore bloomers, a frilly skirt and high-laced shoes, like Jane Fonda in Cat Ballou.

We took off into the night and landed at a bar, where we proceeded to get ripped. Jack had a terrific sense of humor and we had a great time. And despite all the women and men who stopped to stare and ask for autographs, he treated me with respect. He seemed to only have eyes for me.

"Liza, you're so beautiful. I can't believe I didn't call you after we first met." He was so charming. He almost sounded believable. And then the inevitable, "I've got to have you, Liza. Let's go back to my house so we can make love."

Why is it that most men only want to have sex? What happened to the good old-fashioned custom of courting and falling in love? I was thinking about asking him to take me home, but instead I thought, I've been around, what's one more fuck? He sure was a hunk. We left the bar in a hurry and drove over to his house.

As soon as we walked in the door, Jack proceeded to light candles all over the house. I couldn't help but notice how immaculate his home was. Everything was decorated perfectly in beiges and whites, nothing was out of place. It looked like something from *House Beautiful*.

Once the romantic stage was set with flickering candles, he grabbed me and threw me down onto his king-sized bed. His body was heavy on mine as his tongue went for my ear. His right hand was leaning on my hair, and it hurt when he lifted my head. One hand reached for my back. As he searched for the hook on my bra, his tongue continued to lick my ear. Right in the middle of this awkward seduction, I looked up to see a five-foot-high picture of a beautiful, nude woman, her hands modestly covering her private parts. Meanwhile, speaking of private parts, Jack was making his way down my stomach toward mine. I stopped him.

"Hey," I said, pointing to the looming, life-sized picture, "Are you seeing this girl?"

"Not any more. She's just a friend." He continued to nibble.

"Why do you have her picture here?" I put the pressure on.

"It's a nice picture. Look, she's just a good friend. It's you I'm interested in."

I wasn't sure if he was lying, but I felt jealous. I had been caught up in the passion, but the reality was kicking in. I had been lied to by enough other men just to get me into bed. Why should I expect this guy would be any different?

We did make love, though I wondered why I bothered to go through with it. In the morning, he took me home in his Jeep.

Once again, I didn't hear from Jack. Like a bad dream that kept repeating itself, I ran into him about a month later and he invited me out again, this time for a dinner with his producer. I believe he wanted a pretty girl on his arm. It always alleviates rumors of one's sexual orientation to bring along a gorgeous babe.

I went on the date, and again he gave me mixed messages. This night, however, I did something I hadn't done before—I looked past his appearance and I studied his behavior. I noticed that he couldn't stop glancing at himself in the mirror.

That evening, back at his house, Jack sang one song after another to me. He also played his recorded songs, one after another. I eventually found it tedious. I don't mind listening to one song or maybe two, but I've never wanted to make a career out of being a professional audience. He expected me to be intrigued with everything about him. Keeping up with the "ohs" and "ahhs" and adoration was a full-time job I didn't apply for.

When morning came he drove me over to my friend's house, where I was doing a photo shoot. As I got out of the car, he told me he had a surprise for me. Maybe he wasn't so bad after all, I thought. Maybe I just hadn't seen his considerate side. My mind went into its rationalization mode: So what if he's a little erratic, if he's a bit full of himself, if there are rumors about him. He's handsome—and that voice!

Jack ran to the back of the Jeep to get the present. I had mentioned that I liked jewelry. With a smile, he helped me out of the car, holding something behind his back. I strained to peek. Can you imagine the look on my face, the shock, when he held up a color poster of himself!? He had a cocky look on his face as he took out a felt tipped pen and autographed it for me, right there on the hood of the car. What an egotistical creep!

We kissed good-bye and as I walked into the condominium complex on Wilshire, I dumped the poster into a garbage can. We never got together again.

By the way, Jack eventually married the girl in the five-foot nude picture on his wall. I'd like to take this opportunity to tell them both congratulations!

Penthouse Magazine:
Anatomy of a Centerfold Shoot

I've lived a full life. When I watch the talk shows and listen to the guests, I often think to myself, "Been there, done that." Probably one of the more interesting, embarrassing, and uncomfortable experiences I've ever had involved posing as a centerfold for *Penthouse* magazine. Thousands of young women try out for this gig, not realizing the acrobatics they must go through to nail the job.

By now I was twenty-three a bit old for the job; they usually like the girls to be much younger. The payment for posing is five thousand dollars. And there is the added bonus of possibly being chosen "Pet of the Year." That lucky "Pet" wins cash and prizes worth over a million dollars, not to mention acting and modeling offers.

I had originally been asked to pose for *Playboy*, but my girlfriend, Wendy Griffin, insisted I meet her friend, famed photographer Ken Marcus, who shot extensively for *Penthouse*. With hopes of possibly becoming "Pet of the Year," I followed Wendy's advice.

For those who might fantasize that the lovely women in the pages of *Penthouse* are in erotic ecstasy as they expose themselves, I'd like to tell you my experience and let you judge for yourself.

$\mathcal{L}iza$

DAY ONE: THE RINGMASTER

The first meeting with the photographer took place in the living room of Ken Marcus's small home. He liked me right away. I could tell because after the initial greeting he said, "Take off all of your clothes."

You can do all the mental preparation in the world on the way to a meeting like this, but when the moment comes and you're told to strip, it's still embarrassing and awkward. I hesitated, but then decided this is what I was here for. I bit my lip, held my breath and—except for a gold ankle bracelet—took off all my clothes. Ken Marcus seemed pleased. He quickly put on his analytical photographer's hat and began to critique my body.

Glamour photography is an art form. With the intensity of Monet, palate in hand assessing a pond of water lilies, Ken Marcus proceeded. My body was his canvas; by the time I left his home, not an inch of it was left unexamined, unstudied, or unexplored.

"Let's see, we'll have to outline your nipples and color them a different shade here. And over here, we'll have to put a little makeup."

There is no airbrushing in *Penthouse*, as I understand there is in *Playboy*, so you have to have a pretty good physique to begin with. I've always been proud of my body. Yet here, in the home of this world-class photographer, whose meticulously composed magazine spreads have been manhandled by everyone from trash collectors to kings, I admit I felt a bit intimidated. I breathed a sigh of relief when he finally said, "Yes, I'd love to work with you, Liza. You're beautiful."

$\mathcal{L}$*iza*

DAY TWO: THE TEST SHOTS

We next spent a whole day shooting test shots in a huge studio. When I arrived, I was escorted to a room filled with scarves and tops and bras and lace. It was fun to pick from the grab-bag of lingerie, deciding which accessories would flatter my naked body. But what I really wanted was a down parka—the air conditioning felt like an Arctic wind. Shivering, nipples hard, accessories in hand, I was led to a stage and a couch, covered with a white sheet. I proceeded to pose in whatever position I was told to. No human being should ever be in any of these positions, not even for the kinkiest sex. It's fascinating to me that the men who pour over these pictures actually think the women who pose for them are having multiple orgasms while maintaining unnatural, life-threatening positions.

Ken took many photographs of me licking my lips, spreading my legs, arching my back and sighing. But when it was all said and done, I thought we had something special. So did Ken. I got dressed. As I headed out the door, he shouted, "Liza!" I turned. In a manner that he would have used while asking me to pass the salt, busy disassembling his tripod, he called, "Why don't you dye your pubic hair blonde?"

DAYS THREE, FOUR, AND FIVE: THE BIG SHOOT

I'm a natural blonde and my pubic hair is light brown. Most blondes I know have the same coloring. But hey, for five thousand bucks, what's a little peroxide between friends? When the day of the shoot came, I went into the bathroom to check the peroxide job I

110

had given myself. I stared in the mirrored door at my gaudy, orangish-tangerine colored pubes. I looked up close, then backed away, hoping it was the lighting. I took a flashlight and shined it on myself. Every single hair had been dyed the same color as the hair on the heads of one of those boys on "The Partridge Family." I panicked. I was due at the shoot in two hours. I ran to the phone and made two calls, one to my sister, Robin, the other to Wendy. Like characters from *Steel Magnolias*, they rushed over and worked tirelessly to help me achieve a beautiful pale shade of lemon chiffon.

Robin and Wendy saved the day. Once I was blown dry, we headed over to Wendy's condominium. She had a beautiful place, and since Ken Marcus knew her so well, we had decided to do the shoot there.

For three days I posed in every position imaginable. I used every prop, wore every piece of lingerie and balanced myself in every set of high heels I could get my hands on, mostly from Wendy's wardrobe. I really felt glamorous. Wendy stood by my side for the entire time. She helped with the makeup, the hair—I looked gorgeous. During the shoot she even powder-puffed my crotch.

At one point, when I was having a hard time relaxing, Ken began to massage me. He was a good masseur and I enjoyed his touch—until he put his finger down my throat. When I asked what he was doing, which is difficult to do with someone's finger down your throat, he said, "I'm trying to relax your throat muscles. This makes your face relax."

With his finger in my mouth, it felt like some kind of prelude to sex. I told him to stop. Then he told me to masturbate in order to "get into it." He offered me a dildo or a vibrator. I told him he was nuts. I couldn't imagine masturbating in front of him. I found out later that he had done this with many of the girls who posed for him.

At the end of three days, my chastity intact, we bade each other farewell. I took Wendy and Robin to a fancy restaurant in Beverly Hills to celebrate. When my issue came out, we celebrated again. Although I didn't get chosen as "Pet of the Year," my photos ran twice and I was selected by readers as one of the most beautiful girls ever to pose for *Penthouse*. I was proud. For several months I walked around with an air of confidence and self-esteem. But it was only based on this fleeting acknowledgment from others, and it masked the insecurity I really felt. Inside, I believed I was unworthy and bad. So for me, the glamour and the high life my success brought ultimately just led to more drugs. Once again, I started down that all-too-familiar road to self-destruction.

HOLLYWOOD, SEPTEMBER 1989

George Harrison: Something In the Way I Moved

I was, at the time, in need of money to buy drugs and pay my rent, and I had slipped back into prostitution. I hoped to find a new client or two, or perhaps an older, generous man who just liked to look. I went to a Hollywood party.

It started out like a hundred other parties I'd been

to. I was high on cocaine, and I knew that at the very least there would be free drugs available. There always were. When you're young and beautiful in Hollywood, you get invited to many parties like this. The alcohol and cocaine are abundant. The host is usually someone extremely wealthy, a successful film producer, director, or actor. These people like to have as many young, hot-looking babes around as possible to impress their business associates and influential friends. Everyone likes to look at beautiful women, and better yet, fuck them.

George Harrison was sitting in the corner of the library at this particular party, playing a song on the ukulele. Though I was a child during the Beatlemania days, I can still remember watching their movie, *A Hard Day's Night*, on television with my older sister. I knew my mom would have been especially impressed with the fact that I had met someone as famous as he, from her era. What I didn't know was that George Harrison was married. Not that it would have mattered one bit to me at the time. But normally I would have recognized that got-to-have-it-now urgency and figured it out. Many married men attended these parties, and they were easy to spot. Their body language seemed to be shouting, "It's now or never, so hurry up. I have only so much time before I have to pick the kids from school, so let's get on with it."

George Harrison was not one for small talk. This living legend let his needs be known early into our introduction. His first words, cockney accent and all, went something like this, "Come upstairs with me, luv, and give me a blow job." I was surprised at his frankness. But I figured, probably like a thousand women before me, When will I have another chance to blow a Beatle? I decided to comply.

It didn't take long for him to direct my lips to his "British banger." He was definitely not the most romantic man in the world, but I guess a guy like George Harrison doesn't have to be. This superstar has probably had sex with hundreds, if not thousands, of young women all over the world during his stellar career. What I found strange, however, was that the entire time I sucked him off, he kept playing that damned ukulele. My mind was racing. Should I interrupt his strum with small talk? He was acting very matter-of-fact, as if he were transfixed on a rugby match and couldn't be bothered by what I was doing. As he reached orgasm, he ended the song with a grand strum. I didn't know whether to applaud or swallow. I did both.

I have been told that I give some of the best oral sex in Beverly Hills. It was something clients expected from a high-priced call girl. Technique separates the wheat from the chaff, and it separates the sixty-dollar blow jobs from an expensive ten-grand-a-night call girl like I was. Not that I was paid for my services that night, mind you. Money was never discussed.

But I wasn't prepared for what George did next. Without missing a lick (on his ukulele), he started in on another song! No "Thank you," no "That was great," nothing. I didn't have to watch him play for long, because he got up and started walking down the stairs, still fingering that ukulele. I wondered how many women he had done this to. He just took sex for granted. I was left standing there with the taste of him still in my mouth.

Naturally, George didn't even pretend he wanted to

please me. I didn't care because I was on coke and wasn't feeling sexy. It says a lot, however, about George Harrison's arrogance—and the attitude toward women that he shares with many rock stars and other male celebrities—that during the whole experience, he never even asked my name.

Revenge, Bondage Style

After Warren Beatty, if any of the next ten men in my life talked about love, I thought to myself, "Yeah, sure." But after another experience, I learned to even be wary when a guy talked about "fun."

I'll call him Ron, which is not his real name, because I later learned that he's in the Mafia and is not who you'd consider to be a good person. We dated for about a week. We never made love; he was always a gentleman. We'd watch television, have dinner, and just keep each other company.

He was handsome, wealthy, and treated me with the utmost respect. It seemed almost too good to be true. He lived in a mansion in Beverly Hills. After that first week with Ron I began to fantasize that he might be someone I could fall for and maybe marry. I didn't know at the time how he came to have such a gorgeous home. I simply thought I'd never met a man so perfect in my life. I know now that nothing could have been further from the truth.

Occasionally, Ron talked about his former girlfriend. She was a *Playboy* Playmate, which made me a little jealous. He mentioned that they were both into "mild sadomasochism." He talked about what fun they had doing it. For some reason, I didn't put George Santo Pietro's coffee enemas in the category of sado-masochism, but they certainly weren't fun. So I wasn't sure what he was talking about. One evening, Ron turned the television down and said, "Let's do something different." I figured he was talking about having sex for the first time. I said, "Sure". We began to undress each other. He took off my bra and panties and began to caress my body. I felt safe. I trusted him. But the next thing I knew he handcuffed me to his bed with leather restraints, all the while telling me how much I would love it.

After he tied me up, he said, "If things get too rough for you, just say the word *cat* and I'll stop, OK?" I nodded. I was too stunned to object. It had all happened so quickly. Next, he secured my ankles to the bottom posts of the bed. I couldn't move my hands or legs. I wasn't prepared for what came next. He pulled out a hood, the kind that slips over an entire head and has zippers for the mouth, eyes, and nose. The hood also had a chain around the neck. I was beginning to get nervous. As he put the hood on me, he told me to relax. He assured me he wasn't going to hurt me. I tried to relax. But then he began beating me, slowly at first. Each time he hit me he screamed out things like, "You fucking cunt. You deserve to be punished. I'll show you, you whore." The beating soon escalated into a full-force violent beating.

At that time, I didn't consider myself a whore. I was a young girl with a pretty heavy past and I'd turned a few tricks, but I'd never experienced anything like what he was doing to me. When he took out a spiked leather cat-o'-nine-tails and started flailing the thing at me, pounding me and making me bleed, I screamed, "Cat, cat, cat, cat!"

He didn't stop. He just kept viciously, relentlessly attacking me. I could hardly breathe through the mask. He had unzipped the nose area only, so my screams were muffled.

He kept breaking vials of Amyl Nitrite and putting them by my nose to breathe. He also breathed the intoxicating fumes from the crushed vials himself. I knew he could tell I was shouting, "Cat, cat, cat." But the son-of-a-bitch never let up. Only when he had an orgasm while beating me and screaming obscenities at me, did he finally stop. By the time he took off the hood and restraints, I was shaking. I was black and blue and hurt so badly that I couldn't even stand. I lay there bleeding and in shock.

He beat me so severely that I should have been hospitalized. Later I thought about going to an emergency room, but at the time the only thing on my mind was revenge. My opportunity soon came. This sick fuck was apparently so turned on by what he'd done that he asked me if I wanted to do it to him.

With all the Amyl Nitrite he'd given me and the pain I was in, I was really messed up. Lying, I said, "Yeah, I really like it. I think it's fun!"

I then tied his arms and legs to the bed, just like he had done to me. I put the mask on him, leaving just enough of an opening in one of the zippers so he could breathe. Then I went nuts on him. I put Ben Gay all over his balls and his ass and started whipping the shit out of him. I put all of my strength into each attack. I stood over him and used my entire body when I delivered the blows. I was doing this for revenge, but he was loving it. He sure wasn't yelling, "Cat."

Do you have any idea how much Ben Gay burns when applied to sensitive areas? He had to be in extreme pain, at least as much as he had subjected me to. I realized that there was no way I could ever put him in jail for what he had done to me, because I allowed it to happen. I looked at him writhing in pain from the open wounds and the Ben Gay. I said to him, "You'd better watch who you have sex with when you do things like that."

I decided to do something I don't think I would have done under any other circumstances—I left.

I spent the next three days at my mom's house. When she asked about the wounds I told her I had fallen down a flight of stairs. Raising her eyebrows, she said it must have been a very long flight of stairs. I told my sister Robin the truth, though. She just shook her head and helped to nurse my wounds. Robin witnessed so many of the things that happened to me. She felt frustrated that she was powerless to help me save me from myself.

On the third day, this guy called me. I was terrified. I thought he was going to kill me for leaving him like that. But instead, he was calling to ask me on a date! The guy was loony. He actually said, "What you did to me really turned me on. I wasn't found for three days, when the maid came to clean up the house!" He loved the entire ordeal. He couldn't stop calling me. I told him he was a fucking maniac. Obviously, I never saw him again. I felt lucky to be alive.

MULHOLLAND DRIVE, FALL 1989

David Crosby: Wasted On the Way

*T*he following story happened several years ago with David Crosby, so in all fairness I must tell you that I'm not sure about his behavior today. I can only hope that maybe after his liver transplant and drug rehabilitation, he has learned some manners. Back then, however, he made it to my Top Ten Jerk List.

My friend Mario lived in a beautiful home on Mulholland Drive. The view of Los Angeles was spectacular, and he always threw the greatest parties. A music producer, Mario seemed to me to be a wealthy band groupie who loved to have famous people attending his parties. I've met musicians from the Rolling Stones, Bruce Springstein's E Street Band and many more at his parties. One night, in the middle of an impromptu jam session and strumming a song I didn't recognize called "Wasted On the Way," I met David Crosby.

I'm too young to be considered a baby boomer, so I had no idea who this frizzy-haired, bald-headed, very pudgy old man was. Judging by the attention paid to him by the other people at the party, however, it was obvious that he was somebody, and that he thought he was almost godlike. I could tell by the gold ring on his finger that he was married. Since I didn't recognize any of the songs he was playing on his acoustic guitar, I couldn't for the life of me figure out what the fuss was all about.

I wasn't into his music at all, but I was interested

in the cocaine he had. Drugs interested me a lot then. Drugs were my guru. They often dictated who I was with and what I did with them. In this case, though, I knew early on that my interest in him didn't go past the drugs. As I watched him arrange some lines I thought, OK, so he's a little plump. I guess I can try to get into the dimple. But hard as I tried, I couldn't talk myself into ignoring his hair.

A rolled-up hundred-dollar bill hung from his nose as he sniffed his way to nirvana. For every three lines he did, I was offered one. But I didn't mind; I was happy he was sharing at all. After a while, we must have gone through a thousand dollars worth of cocaine. Actually, he probably went through about seven hundred and fifty dollars' worth while I went through two hundred and fifty dollars' worth—but who's counting?

Eventually the cocaine ran out and he offered to drive me home. I figured, why not? The drugs were gone. There wasn't any real reason for me to stay around this party. I jumped into his Corvette and off we went.

He took a left at Beverly Glen, heading into the San Fernando Valley instead of going to the right—the route that would have taken us to my home in West-wood. I asked where we were going and he casually told me he had to pick something up at his hotel in Encino. He assured me it wouldn't take long, and that I could wait in the car.

As we cruised down Ventura Boulevard, he began groping my thigh. He wasn't a gentle man. In fact, he was rather harsh and abrasive. I took his sticky fingers and put them back on the steering wheel. He didn't push. I felt relieved.

As we drove up to the Hilton Hotel in Encino, he acted very cool. He parked and got out of the car. He walked to the front entrance of the hotel, stopped, and then turned back toward me. When he reached the car, he motioned me to roll down the window.

"Why don't you come in with me?" he suggested.

"I'd rather wait, if you don't mind."

"I do mind. Somebody might see you here, recognize my car, and tell my wife. How about coming in for a minute? I'm in room number 204. Just follow behind me, act like we're not together, and I'll let you in." After a second he added, "Remember, don't look at anybody. Especially the guy behind the desk. He knows me and my wife."

I didn't want to go inside, but I bought his line and didn't want him to get into trouble with his wife. It seemed like such a small request.

"All right, I'll follow you," I said. "But please don't take long. I really want to get home." He nodded.

I followed him into his room. He picked up the telephone and called somebody. I think he wanted me to believe that he really had important business to take care of, but it just sounded like small talk to me. While he was on the telephone, he was looking me over. Finally, after chatting about the Alcoholics Anonymous meeting he had missed and a few other things, he hung up. He then turned to me in a very matter-of-fact manner. His fat face turned red and his tiny lips puckered together as he delicately queried, "So are we going to fuck, or what?"

I was speechless at first. It's both puzzling and disgusting to me that these rock stars think all they have to do is get it up and anyone they happen to point to owes it to them to take care of them.

I thought to myself, I'd rather fuck Pee-Wee Herman. A stunned silence followed as I collected myself and said, "Of course not."

After getting over the initial shock of my not saying, "Yeah baby, do me now," he stared at me and in a very intimidating manner said, "Look, babe, I didn't drive all the way out here for nothing!"

"I told you no, and I mean it." I was firm.

"Do you know who I am?" he shot back.

"Yeah, some fat-faced schmuck with frizzy hair." I then repeated my request to be taken home.

He grabbed me by the arm and dragged me out of the hotel room, down the hall, and through the lobby. The check-in clerk's mouth dropped wide open when he saw this rock icon dragging a young girl through the lobby and out to the parking lot.

"Get in the car, bitch. You're going home."

David Crosby threw me into the Corvette, revved it up, and screeched out of the parking lot. We sped down Ventura Boulevard at 85 miles an hour. I was scared. I was praying a policeman would pull us over, but it never happened.

"Where did you say you live, bitch?" He was very hostile and degrading.

I proceeded to give him directions as he raced over Coldwater Canyon, through Beverly Hills to Westwood. I was terrified as he took each hairpin turn in the canyon and careened into the oncoming lanes. He was driving like a madman.

When we arrived at my house, he didn't open my car door. He just stared straight ahead. I was shaking as I let myself out. He slammed his foot on the accelerator and took off, almost taking me with him. I jumped out of the way, and the passenger door slammed shut with the forward thrust of the car.

I had nightmares that night. It took me a couple of hours to come down from the sheer terror of the evening. The next morning a friend of mine called to tell me that David Crosby had just told him, "I gave that little cunt a good scare. You should have seen her, the fucking bitch."

Like many guys in this town who expect sex just because they are celebrities, David Crosby has a hard time with rejection from a woman. It's a shock. For my part, I was just glad I didn't fuck one more guy I didn't want to fuck.

Billy Idol: Hot Chocolate Fix

I was walking down Rodeo Drive in Beverly Hills with my girlfriend Nikki, when suddenly a very plain, dark-haired man in his early forties approached us. The first words out of his mouth were, "Would you like to meet Billy Idol?" Nikki and I looked at each other. It sounded intriguing. We listened as he explained, "You're really beautiful girls. I'm personally handling Billy. I'm his producer. I'm sure he'd love to meet you. Can you come with me?"

Nikki and I talked for a moment. She was a fan of Billy's, although I couldn't care less about him. After discussing whether or not we had anything better to do, we decided, "Why not?" So we and the producer drove to Billy Idol's suite at the Beverly Hills Hotel.

I'd been to the Beverly Hills Hotel bungalows before, but my last visit involved a "fee for service" arrangement. We walked down the maze of sidewalks,
past individual buildings that have served as tempo-
rary hideaways for many big names. The gardens
were immaculately manicured and beautifully lit at
night, with colored spotlights shining on towering
palm trees. It is a romantic hotel.

Billy's bungalow was decorated in peaches and
greens and consisted of a main living room, two bedrooms, and two bathrooms. Billy has hangers-on like
every rock star, so we weren't surprised to see his bungalow loaded with people.

Billy Idol has very poor eyesight. When we were
introduced to him, he searched for his glasses so he
could take a good look. It was obvious to us that he
had been up partying for several days. His appearance
was nothing like his music videos. He was shabby and
disheveled, his hair was all matted and he seemed to be
drooling.

Nikki and I, on the other hand, looked hot. We were
wearing sexy little bra tops and tights, with high
heeled shoes and leather jackets. Billy kept staring at
me. Nikki was beginning to get upset—she was the one
with the crush on this guy, not me. I really didn't care.
After several minutes of silence and some intense staring and drooling, Billy mumbled something inaudible.
I finally said, "What?" He tried again. I thought he
said, "I want some hot chocolate."

None of his hangers-on moved. He repeated, "I
want some hot chocolate." Still nobody moved. So I
took it upon myself to order some hot chocolate for
him from room service. As I walked over to the telephone, Billy staggered into one of the bathrooms.

We waited for the hot chocolate to arrive. After a while, I decided to see what had happened to Billy. The bathroom door was open ever so slightly. I knocked. There was no answer. I began to speak to him through the opening. "Billy? Are you all right?"

"Come in, love," he said softly.

I didn't know what to expect as I pushed the door open and stepped in. I was agahst at what I saw. Standing in front of the mirror, with a small rubber tube wrapped around and a syringe sticking into his arm, was Billy Idol. He had just shot up and had left the needle in. It was obvious that he was riding on a heroin high. His moon eyes looked at me and in a perfect British accent he said, "I'm fine, dear."

I'd seen people shooting up before, but I'd never shot up myself. The whole scene makes me really uncomfortable. I've known girls who are hooked on needles, and they have horrible bruises on their arms and ankles from their never-ending search for new veins to assault with poisons. I smiled at Billy and nodded as I backed out of the door. I said, "Good. That's good."

I quickly found Nikki and told her that I wanted to leave. She was reluctant because she was hoping to get better acquainted with her hero. I hated to burst her bubble, but this guy was bad news. As we were making our way out the door, Billy emerged from the bathroom smiling. He seemed to be listening to a fifty-piece orchestra that only he could hear.

"Thank you, dear, for ordering my hot chocolate," he slurred. Not missing a beat he added, "Can I have your telephone number?"

Nikki was livid as I gave him my number. I did it just to be polite, but I would never go out with him.

I've done a lot of stupid things in my life, but I would never go out with someone who shot up.

The following day Billy called several times, asking me to go out with him. I told him I was busy, and I never heard from him again. I felt sorry for him, but thank God I had enough sense not to be drawn into that scene. What I was already into was bad enough.

Whenever I pass the Beverly Hills Hotel, order hot chocolate, or watch Billy Idol on MTV, I can't help but think of him as I remember him—standing in the bathroom with a needle in his arm.

HOLLYWOOD, 1989

Madam Liza: My Lowest Point

Being a coke whore and a prostitute is not pretty. It is sad. I should know; I was both.

My first prostitution experience was for love, my second was a mistake, but after that, it was always for money to buy more drugs and for the sheer, wild danger of it. I was really rebellious—I wanted to cross the line. The fact that it was illegal and dangerous was part of what appealed to me.

Each time I sold myself, it was harder to not do it the next time. My willingness to sell my body evolved to a great extent from my long time willingness to give it away for free. I gave it away because I wanted the attention. Being around famous guys made me feel like a celebrity. It was fun. There were times when I felt used, but I so much wanted to be loved and cared about that I was afraid to say no to anybody.

There are an astounding number of call girls in this city. Heidi Fleiss and Madam Alex are just the tip of the iceberg; the demand for high-priced girls is quite staggering. A lot of the sex that rich men and celebrity clients want is weird, sick, and sadistic. Sometimes the sicker the stuff, the more they will pay.

A friend of mine who was close to Madam Alex told me about a couple of prostitutes who were hired by Sylvester Stallone. He would pay ten to fifteen thousand dollars a girl for one night. These two girls I know, a blonde and a brunette, used to go over to his house. He would have them sit on a Plexiglas platform over his bed. Then he would lie down on the bed to watch. He would tell them to make love to each other and to piss and shit on each other, and as he watched them, he'd jerk off.

That kind of sick stuff goes on every night in Hollywood, and that was the world I eventually sank into. Probably the lowest point for me was when I began to freebase cocaine. I lost myself completely then. It is a very bad drug, and you lose all sense of what is right or good for you.

One of the times I was basing, I decided I was going to be a madam. I knew a lot of people in the record business. Andy Howitt, who worked for Geffen Records, asked me to find some girls for Steven Tyler of the Aerosmith band. I got three girls I knew were prostitutes and the record company paid the girls through me and I got a couple of tickets to an Aerosmith concert. Tyler wanted the girls to get dressed up in bondage equipment and whip and tie him. After they whipped him, he'd whip them and fuck them.

Then the record company wanted to cut a deal with me to keep them supplied with girls. With the amount of base I was doing then, however, I was too fucked up to handle it. But I didn't have the heart for it anyway. Later I heard that Heidi was working with Geffen Records.

Each time I sunk lower—like being a madam and not just selling myself, but selling other girls—it hit me hard. I'd feel worse about myself and I'd get more and more messed up with drugs to deal with how I felt. I felt awful selling other girls, even ones who said they loved being a prostitute. To me, it was cheap, dirty sex. It wasn't real, it wasn't loving. It wasn't emotional. When I started to get free of drugs, I finally got free of prostitution.

I met a guy that I've been seeing for a long time now. He's younger than me, and he's a good person. It's been great, though there've been hard times. It's almost impossible for me, after what I've been through, to really feel safe with another person.

Every day is a struggle. But I'm on the road back.

BEVERLY HILLS, FALL 1989

Don Dolores: Cross-Dressing Diva

*J*ust before I started to get my life together, I had one more fling—and almost lost my life in the process. I met a man, whom I will call Don Dolores, through two people: my pimp, Al Black, and an ex-boyfriend, Kenny Austin, son of the then-head of Warner Bros. Records. I was completely taken with this man's charm, style, and ability to show me the greatest time money could buy, including all the drugs I needed. Don really helped me get even more addicted to freebasing cocaine. It's the same drug that comedian Richard Pryor was using when he caught on fire and burned a good portion of his body. I can understand how it might have happened. I've been there.

The freebasing ritual involves rock cocaine, a spoon, a lighter, and a bong pipe. You put the rock cocaine in a spoon and hold the flame under it. You melt the cocaine down and then put it into the bong to smoke it. It is a highly addictive habit and one that Don had been doing nonstop for years. Don and I were both completely drugged out back then. I guess he was happy to have found a woman to share his life and drugs with, so he asked me to marry him. In my drug-induced haze, I couldn't imagine a more perfect union. I accepted.

Don is one of the heirs to a very big cosmetic company. But he has been basing for so long that he's simply bonkers—more than one slice shy of a full loaf. From the first date with him, however, when he brought out the biggest stash of dope I'd ever seen, I was so impressed that I couldn't have cared less about his personality flaws. One major problem is that he's paranoid from the drugs. Determined to get to people before they get him, he has bodyguards protecting him twenty-four hours a day. Another quirk is that he often dresses up like a woman. But he could have had a sex-change operation for all I cared; the only thing that mattered to me were the drugs.

Three months before our wedding day, we drove down the Royal Palm–lined Beverly Hills streets in his Rolls Royce, house-hunting.

"We have three mansions to see today, Liza," Don

said. "I want you to tell me which one you want. Remember, if you don't find one you like, we're set to look again tomorrow. The realtor has scheduled a helicopter for us, so we can take a look from the air."

I picked out a mansion that day. He paid cash. I thought I was in love. That night was one of many nights he let his hair down, so to speak, and got into his cross-dressing fetish.

"Do you think I should wear the pearls or the ruby necklace, dear?" Don would take on a woman's voice when he was "coming out" for the evening.

I rummaged through his jewelry box and pulled out some divine pearl-and-ruby clip earrings. "Try them both," I suggested. I handed him the expensive jewelry and continued looking through the cache, which was easily worth a hundred thousand dollars. When it came to his indulgences, money was no object. "Let me see, I think the pearls do wonders for your complexion. Who was it who once said, 'With a string of pearls and thin hips, a woman can get any man she desires'?"

"Claire Booth Luce."

"Ah, yes."

I stood there smiling, wondering how something as absurd as this could become standard fare in our relationship.

"Take some pictures of me, darling. I love looking at myself." He handed me the Polaroid camera and told me the correct angle from which to shoot. I snapped seven pictures and handed them back to him. After oohing and ahhing, he tossed them into the top drawer of his dresser.

Don Dolores couldn't make love—he was too strung out. I believe he had had this affliction for years. The truth is, we were both badly strung out. One day, while I was with Don, I went over to my parents' house. My sister, Robin, was there. She looked at me in horror. I was twitching, my motor functions had disintegrated from the drugs. I had also lost a lot of weight. Robin was determined to make me see what was happening to me. She took me to a mirror and stood next to me.

"Look at us both, Liza. Who looks sick and who doesn't?"

She looked normal. I looked like a skeleton. It shocked me. I started to cry and couldn't stop crying.

Robin took me to a rehabilitation clinic and checked me in. After a while I started drying out and finally began to breathe sane air here on planet earth. Until then, I was definitely off with Don in another orbit.

During my absence, Don Dolores decided that I was out to get him. He hired a hit man to take me out. The hit man came to my parents' home, where my brother, a martial arts expert, kicked the gun out of the assailant's hand before he could shoot me. Sometime after that, I made the trek over to Don's house and began a four-hour ordeal, trying to get through to his thick, freebase-damaged brain that I hadn't done him wrong. I'm here today because I was able to convince Don that he had the wrong girl. I told him I was away drying out, so I couldn't have been out to get him. Fortunately, I resisted getting back into freebase hell that night, and once again I walked away with my life.

WESTWOOD, 1995

A Grateful Survivor

I wouldn't be entirely truthful if I told you I wasn't writing this book, at least in part, for monetary reasons. I do have another reason for writing it, however, and to me it is a very important one. If my experiences can help young girls and their parents recognize the steps in the long, downward spiral of drugs, prostitution, and abuse, if it can help others make changes in their lives so that they may never have to go where I've been, then my life and the writing of this book will have been worthwhile.

Parents often aren't aware that when children act out, it is usually to get approval or attention. They are seeking love. If my parents had recognized and understood my pain, and early on given me unconditional love and acceptance, I believe my life may have turned out differently. But in my misguided attempts to let them know I needed their nurturing and their guidance, I started out on a slow road to hell.

My mother was the kind of person who tried to pretend all was well. My dad was usually too busy to care. He tried to show love by acknowledging my beauty, by pointing out that my looks were the best, and just about the only, thing I had going for me, perhaps along with acting talent. But what he thought were compliments made me feel I had nothing but my looks to rely on.

When I started doing drugs, staying out late, getting into trouble, I wish my parents had taken the time to sit down with me, tell me they cared, and help me build a direction for my life. Later my mother tried many times to help. But if that effort had been made earlier, before I had sunk so low, it might have been more effective.

When a close relative molested me at the age of twelve, I told my parents and they didn't believe me. And so, when the prostitute who was in my father's porno film and her friend raped me at the age of thirteen, I was not anxious to run and tell anyone. I thought I would not be believed. When my reality was questioned by my parents, I stopped trusting them. I turned to drugs and eventually to prostitution to support my drug habit.

Like most children, I simply wanted to be believed, to be needed, to be loved. I had nothing to gain by lying about a relative having molested me. I only wanted help, so it would never to happen again. Life is difficult enough, particularly in a place like Hollywood. But when you have disbelievers in your own camp, it is almost impossible.

I also hope this book will help young girls who might already be into drugs, prostitution, or abusive relationships with men. My message for them is that it is never too late to turn your life around. Drugs are so deceptive. They appear to be an escape from pain, but in reality, drugs are a deep well. The deeper you fall in that well, the harder it is to climb up and out. The walls are slippery, and they get more and more difficult to scale each time you try. The time to catch yourself is in the beginning.

People who do drugs will always try to get you to join them. Misery loves company, and drug users are miserable—if not at the moment of the high, then certainly afterward, when the guilt of their actions comes flooding in. There wasn't a waking moment when I was doing drugs that I didn't ask myself over and over, "What am I doing to myself?"

Real friends do not give their friends drugs. Men often try to control women through drugs. Drugs are a big part of the prostitute/pimp equation. Too often in my past, I mistook an act of control for an act of kindness.

I have vowed to myself many times to never go back to drugs. Yet sometimes I am drawn back into the vicious circle, usually by "friends" who are still using. I regret what I have put my family through. They have stood by helplessly, watching me self-destruct. I was lucky, however, that they never gave up on me. They have been an important part of why I have pulled through so far. But I've seen hundreds of other women in drug rehabs who haven't been as fortunate as me.

Men who only like women if they have sex with them are not friends either. I wish I had learned at a younger age that if a situation feels uncomfortable, I shouldn't stay in it. Often I had a feeling of apprehension, but I ignored it. I wish I had said in those moments, "Let me take some time to think about this." I wish I hadn't made so many decisions in the pressure of the moment. When Timothy Hutton brought his boyfriend over to make love to me, I should have left— and there are a dozen other times in my life I should have done the same.

In the past, I never felt I could speak in terms of right and wrong, but today I can. I feel it is right to respect your body, your mind, and your soul. It is wrong to allow yourself to be used, drugged, manipulated, controlled, or abused in any way. I now realize that just because someone is famous or powerful, it doesn't mean I owe them sex. Having sex with someone never made anyone respect or like me more. In fact, it mostly did the opposite, though I didn't realize it at the time. The false sense of importance or acceptance I might have felt in being with some famous guy was too often over as soon as he went on to his next conquest. When he dumped me or never called, my self-esteem would plummet to new lows, and I would reach for more drugs to try to escape the pain.

I wish I could talk to each and every young girl who is on that downward spiral and try to encourage her to begin to love herself. I see beautiful young women on the arms of their pimps and I want to say, "Please, stop your destructive life. Start respecting yourself."

I'm lucky. I got out. Many of the friends I knew who got caught up in drugs and prostitution are either dead, in jail—like my friend Linda, whose story is next—or so far down they literally have no hope for a normal life.

The hardest thing in my life has been to forgive myself. I know I messed up. Fortunately, I have made some progress and am now on a path to an uncertain future, but one I know will be a whole lot better than my past. I'm older, steadily wiser, and certainly happier. All those kinky, degrading sexual experiences are behind me. I haven't done prostitution in years and, although I haven't been drug-free for more than a year at a time yet, I'm thankful for every day I live a productive, drug-free life. It has been, and still is, a long, hard road.

Sometimes I look in the mirror. I see those scars on my wrists from my suicide attempts. I see a woman who has paid her dues. It's been hard to admit in these pages just how much I have hurt myself. But I also see a woman aching for a normal life, for a better future, and for the self-love I need to get there. I see a survivor—and for that, I am very grateful.

Linda

HEIGHT:	5'8"
HAIR:	Blonde
EYES:	Blue
WEIGHT:	125
PROFESSION:	Call girl
BORN:	Newport Beach, California
HOBBIES:	Traveling
EDUCATION:	UCLA; did not complete degree.
FIRST SEXUAL EXPERIENCE:	At fifteen, with an eighteen year old.
GOALS AND DESIRES:	To go to school to become a dental assistant.
SEXUAL FANTASY:	To make love with a woman . . . oops, I already did that!
DRUGS:	Cocaine, Quaaludes, alcohol.
HAPPIEST MEMORY:	Being released from jail.
WORST EXPERIENCE:	Being busted by an undercover officer for prostitution.
SEX PARTNERS:	James Caan, Don Henley, Glenn Frey, Dennis Hopper, and more.

THE DIARIES

For the Record

It seems like a lifetime ago, when I would casually board a plane for Europe or New York, wearing a two-thousand-dollar Chanel suit and hundred-dollar-an-ounce perfume, thinking about the millionaire I'd been hired to spend time with. I thought the party would never end. The drugs, the attention, my popularity. There wasn't enough time in the day to take care of all the men who wanted me.

For those of you who believe in Hollywood fantasies such as the movie *Pretty Woman*, I can assure you, that fairy tale doesn't exist. I have actually lived the life Julia Roberts lived with Richard Gere, her john. I've had the best of everything—jewelry, clothing, the finest cars, fancy hotels, great restaurants, the works. But when the party's over, the party is over. Sooner or later the drugs run out, the money runs dry, your novelty fades, the wife comes back from that visit to her sister's . . . and you go home empty and alone, with nothing more than the memory of a good time, if the drugs don't take that away from you, too.

I've been asked what I think about when I have sex with a customer and if I can differentiate between a john and a boyfriend. I may not give the answer you expect. The truth is, I can't differentiate between the two. My mind always seems to drift. I used to think about the drugs I'd buy with the money I was making. I'd barely feel a man touch me; my mind would be on holiday. Sex was automatic. Now, I'm preoccupied wondering if I will ever be able to feel again the way I felt before I resorted to using my body as a means to get drugs and money.

When I saw *Pretty Woman*, I thought, another Hollywood male fantasy. The worst part about the movie is that is gives the false impression to young girls that it's even remotely possible for those romantic dreams to become a reality. What happened in *Pretty Woman* only happens in the movies. In real life, you're left with track marks, arrest records, and bad dreams. And if you're lucky, someday you get out alive.

COLDWATER CANYON, SPRING 1981

Off Track

$\mathcal{M}$any people believe that young women who get caught up in drugs and prostitution come from poor, broken homes. For me that's only partly true. I grew up in Newport Beach, where beautiful homes and expensive cars were commonplace. My parents were divorced when I was young, but I was a very normal, very bright, very ambitious girl. I lived with my mother, a grade school teacher. I missed my father and rarely saw him after he remarried. During high school I worked two jobs, saved for my college education, and even bought my own car. My goal was to become a lawyer, and I also dreamed of getting married and raising a family. When I won a full scholarship to UCLA, I felt like I was on my way.

I arrived at UCLA for my freshman year determined to start on the road to becoming a corporate attorney. I was eighteen years old, tall, thin, with beautiful blonde hair and my mother's gorgeous smile and knockout figure.

I wasn't prepared for what hit me in Los Angeles. Everywhere I went, I began to meet thirty- to forty-five-year-old men who had beautiful homes and cars and all of the material trappings I admired while growing up in Newport Beach. These men were not only willing to share their possessions with me, they actually stood in line to do so. They didn't care about my education, only my body.

I met one man named Freddy and soon became the object of his affection. Freddy owned racehorses and ran several businesses. A Rolls Royce and a Mercedes were in his garage. He was an entrepreneur with a passion for the good life, which included very young women and drugs.

One Friday night I drove up to Freddy's Coldwater Canyon home in my Volkswagen, ready to accompany him on a promised trip to Palm Springs. When I arrived at his house he said, "Linda, have I got a surprise for you!" It turned out that the surprise was several ounces of cocaine. The street value was in the range of several thousand dollars.

That night Freddy introduced me to the world of

coking up and freebasing. We never made it to Palm Springs. It was the beginning of the end of my dreams and aspirations. I went from wanting to be a high-powered, independent professional woman in the legal world to slowly sliding into the quicksand of drug addiction and, eventually, prostitution.

Once, the most important part of my day was cramming for a test. Now I was cramming powder up my nose. The former innocent days when I was flirting with a UCLA football player seemed like a lifetime away from my new existence. The euphoria I felt from the drugs was electrifying at first. Then I'd fade into a dreamlike existence, my spirit and soul numb. I would lay in a drugged-out stupor, staring at the ceiling mirror as Freddy did perverse things to my body.

For a short time my life seemed beautiful. Everything seemed simple. Drugs were my life, and I had a man who was supplying me with these drugs. Sometimes I'd still manage to make it down the hill to UCLA, eyes glassy, body wired. I was pathetic, but I didn't know it. I attended classes until Freddy encouraged me to stop.

In my clouded state of mind, life seemed carefree and perfect. At least, that is, until the day the drugs ran out. I came home one evening after visiting a friend, and Freddy announced that he didn't have any drugs for us.

"No drugs Linda. Sorry."

Since the day we began taking drugs together, it never occurred to me what life would be like without them. I just assumed they'd keep on coming. At first I tried to keep my composure.

"What do you mean?" I calmly asked.

"I mean exactly what I said. No drugs."

"Okay, fine."

"I know you'll leave me now, Linda. You'll find someone else who can give you drugs."

"What?"

"I always knew I'd lose you if I couldn't supply you with drugs."

"Why are you saying such a ridiculous thing?" I was incensed. How insulting, I thought, to say that I was only with him for drugs! But I did leave him. I used the excuse that he was a fool for accusing me of using him, but in fact, he was right.

L'ERMITAGE HOTEL, FALL 1982

Mr. Wimbledon: 40/Love

*M*y introduction to drugs had been extremely unrealistic. Since Freddy had been providing everything I needed in the drug department, I hadn't quite realized that it took money to keep up a drug habit. At the time, I took it for granted that most wealthy men took drugs and were happy to share them with the woman they dated. So when I had the opportunity to meet a famous tennis player and his friend, I jumped at the chance. Just say the magic five-letter word— *drugs*—and I was off to the races. Once again I was high enough to believe that the party would never end.

"Mr. Wimbledon" and his friend, Tony Gobel, were staying at L'Ermitage Hotel and wanted to call some hookers. My girlfriend, who had been partying with them, suggested they call me instead. At this point, I'd never had sex for money.

Mr. Wimbledon, Tony, my girlfriend, and I drove around in a big limousine, sniffing cocaine and drinking champagne. It was marvelous—the discos, the night life, even the sex. The only problem was that I fell in love with Tony. I liked everything about him. I thought the feeling was mutual until the day they left and the party was suddenly over. Tony and Mr. Wimbledon were off to the next city, and I was left with a broken heart. I told myself it would be the last time I'd get personally involved with a married man.

I had given up my law-school dreams for the pleasure of the moment. I had taken others' dreams as my own. But men like Mr. Wimbledon and Tony had different priorities: have fun, then move on. I foolishly expected the party to last forever. And each time, when it ended, I was left even more alone and disillusioned, searching for the next high.

LAS VEGAS AND PARIS, 1983

Adnan Khashoggi: My First Trick

I never made a conscious decision to become a prostitute; in fact, I never really considered myself a prostitute or a whore. I chose to do it because it was an opportunity to make large amounts of money and to travel. At first I thought, this is cool. It's fun.

My first trick occurred when a girlfriend of mine called me from Las Vegas. I asked her what she was doing there and she said, "I'm a guest of Adnan Khashoggi. He's one of the richest men in the world." She explained to me that there were about ten girls there, in one of the big hotels. They could charge anything they wanted, order anything they wanted from room service, and they each got a thousand dollars a day.

"It's so much fun. You've got to come."

I was staying at my mother's house at the time. I told her about the offer and the chance to make a thousand bucks a day.

"I'll have no part of this," she said. "If you want to go you'll have to take a cab to the airport."

I did go. And I met Khashoggi. He seemed to be in the process then of meeting lots of women. Occasionally he would really take to someone, and he lavish hugh sums of money and gifts on her. I guess I wasn't one of them. He was very charming and gentle to me, but I wasn't with him long. I did, however, come home from that trip with several thousand dollars in cash. I thought, wow, that was easy.

My opportunity to really get into "the life" followed shortly afterward. The same friend who invited me to join Khashoggi's parade of young girls told me about Cathy and Al Black. I was informed that they had connections with wealthy men from all over the world. They would set up jobs and, even though they took fifty percent, the money was good and you got to travel. What the hell, I thought. I needed money—for drugs, my car, my rent. At the time, I was too stupid to realize what I was doing to myself.

I went up to the Blacks' house in Coldwater Canyon. They asked me if I wanted to go on a trip to Europe: I'd get five hundred dollars a day and would stay in the best hotels. I was jazzed; I'd never been to Europe. Before the trip, however, they wanted me to see a client—sort of a test. I got dressed up and they dropped me off at this guy's place. I was with him for a few hours. The sex was not really significant. It was the first time I had slept with someone I didn't know for money.

Then off to Europe we went, about ten girls and Cathy Black. The first stop was Paris. We had the days to ourselves, and at night we worked. We would be taken to these parties where the men were all Arabs. They were not particularly attractive, but I guess they were rich. More than sex, they wanted to be entertained. They'd put on Arab music and we would dance and talk and joke around with them. There were usually hashish or Quaaludes and plenty to eat and drink. Then, at the end of the evening, we would pair off and go to different rooms with them. The sex part usually lasted about ten minutes or so. It was just off with the clothes, a little head, and then doing it. By the time we got down to the physical involvement, I was usually in a pretty good mood from the drugs, the alcohol, the partying. But during the sex acts, I was always thinking about something else. I guess they call it dissociating. It was the way I escaped from having any feelings about what I was doing. And I never, from the first time on, had an orgasm with a client. Of course, I was great at faking it.

Before the trip, the Blacks had promised that we'd come home with about ten thousand dollars each. I ended up with three thousand plus a few tips, but I didn't mind too much. After all, I thought, I got to see Paris.

SAN DIEGO AND L.A., SPRING 1983

Losing It All

*A*l and Cathy Black, were definitely high-class pimps. At the time, they had the best connections and the most beautiful women in Los Angeles, and I was among their favorites. But they were not nice people, and playing their game meant playing by their rules.

I had that *Pretty Woman* fantasy in those days: the next trick might be the one who would take me away from a life of prostitution. And so, two hours after receiving a call from Cathy and Al Black one day, I sat on an airplane bound for San Diego and fantasized about what my client might be like. I was told he was an Arab and they often dressed in the costume of their native country—white cotton gowns, headdresses, breads, the works.

When I stepped off of the plane I looked around for a man dressed like this. I wasn't prepared for the sharply dressed older gentleman in the custom-tailored Italian silk suit who took my arm. "Sam," a man with an important position in the Saudian Arabian government at the time, was immediately taken with me, even though I was the same age as his youngest daughter.

Sam talked a lot that night and in the nights to come. "My family uses me for money," he complained. "Only money. That's all they think I'm good for. None of them cares about me at all."

I listened. I looked into this lonely man's beautiful

149

dark eyes and something inside told me that this guy might really be different.

We did drugs and drank a lot those first two days we spent together. The sex part was standard. He entered me, pumped a few times, and it was over. He thought he satisfied me, which made him feel good. But our time together was really more like an extended therapy session than a wild sex orgy.

Shortly after I returned to Los Angeles, the phone rang and it was Cathy Black.

"Listen, Linda, I don't know what you did to Sam in San Diego, but he's mad about you. He wants to see you tonight."

"Fine."

"And Linda?"

"Yes?"

"I upped the price to fifteen hundred. Show the man a good time; I think he's falling in love."

My heart was racing. It felt so good to be desired. I felt like I was going on a second date with a boyfriend. I took a bath and put on sexy lingerie. I arrived on schedule. Sam was there to greet me, bearing two dozen yellow roses. I was on cloud nine—he seemed to really care about me. Two days later, we were both on a flight to Las Vegas. There, he bought me a Piaget Polo watch worth twelve thousand dollars, some clothes, and presents for my mother. Sam treated me like a princess. I wanted this feeling to last forever. When I returned to Los Angeles, I discovered that Sam had ordered a beautiful white Mercedes convertible for me to pick up at the Newport Beach Mercedes dealer.

I never called Cathy Black again. Sam took such good care of me: he called me often, gave me money, and whenever possible came to see me or had me fly somewhere to meet him. It was like a fairy tale romance.

Then something terrible happened. I was robbed at gunpoint while on a drug buy as a favor for a friend, in a not-so-nice neighborhood near downtown Los Angeles. To this day, I think Al and Cathy Black set up that robbery. One minute I was driving a Mercedes, the next I was penniless on a street corner, grateful that I had gotten out alive. My car had been stolen, as had my new watch and the twenty-thousand-dollar sable coat Sam had just given me. Hysterical, I called my mother to rescue me. When she came to pick me up, I tried to explain what happened. She was very upset.

"You're living too dangerous a lifestyle," she told me. "You're part of the underworld."

When we got to the house, she called Sam. She knew he was my boyfriend, but she didn't know how I had met him. After she talked to him, I took the phone and reluctantly explained what had happened. I was embarrassed, but he was understanding and wanted to help. He also wanted me closer to him.

"Why don't you pick any place in the world you'd like to live—Paris, London, Amsterdam—and I'll set up up in an apartment and you can go to school. You can get out of Los Angeles."

Could this really be my knight in shining armor?

"Talk it over with your mother. She can come with you to get you settled. Let me know where you want to go."

Paris. That's where I wanted to go. Almost overnight, my mother and I were flying first-class to Europe. It was like a dream. We stayed in a suite at the Ritz. Sam gave me twenty thousand dollars for a shopping spree, and I gave my mother five thousand of it.

We had a fabulous time. Then Sam and I went on a trip to the south of France. I loved Monte Carlo, and that's where I decided to stay. It was like a wild movie, and I was the star. One day I was in Los Angeles being robbed at gunpoint, the next I was living a fantasy life in a penthouse apartment in Villa de Copra.

MONACO, SUMMER 1983

Stephano Caseraghi Meets His Bride

*I*n Monaco my life changed completely. I was really trying to get myself together, and had quit drinking and doing drugs. I joined a gym and worked out. Everything I needed was provided by Sam. I spent my time decorating the apartment in my favorite style, art deco. I covered the beautiful fourteen-foot walls in a rich fabric, and upholstered the black lacquer furniture in plush velour. I put expensive Erte art on the walls. My bedroom was something Barbra Streisand or Joni Mitchell would have been proud to call their own.

For a time, my only connection with Sam was clandestine phone calls and checks that came regularly in the mail. He rarely had time to visit.

I was living the high life in a magical place. Word traveled fast in the upper echelon where I now dwelt: a rich American girl had moved to town. Nobody knew how I got my money; they assumed I came from a wealthy family. I wore jewelry from Bulgari and Cartier and clothing from Chanel and Yves Saint Laurent. My appearance attested to the illusion that I was independently wealthy, and I wasn't about to burst anyone's bubble with the truth.

I met Stephano Caseraghi one evening at a club. He was young and handsome and came from a wealthy family. He was immediately taken with me, or perhaps with the money he thought I had. Unbeknownst to him, of course, I was a kept woman, a former hooker from Beverly Hills. For three months I dated Stephano. Apparently his parents were footing his bill, but according to him they were cheap and didn't take care of all of his monetary needs. Stephano and I had a lot of fun together. He took me on yachts and to many parties. He wanted to be seen everywhere with me; we were known as a couple. I didn't feel like I was cheating on Sam because I never slept with Stephano.

One party Stephano took me to was hosted by a very wealthy single woman. Her name was Princess Caroline. Her home was located in "Old Monaco"—I was surprised at how small it was, but the furnishings were elegant. When Stephano and I met the princess for the first time, I could tell that my handsome boyfriend was attracted to our hostess. That night, as Stephano held my hand, I sensed Princess Caroline was also attracted to him. I knew Stephano's appeal was enhanced because I was on his arm. Stephano looked up at Caroline, who had just given each of us a glass of wine. After their eyes met, he quickly looked over to me.

"Linda darling, tomorrow night I have a surprise for you," he confided.

Could it be a proposal of marriage? We'd been dating for months now. He had hinted at marriage before. My mind raced. What if he did actually propose?

My first thought was, how can I tell him about the

secret I've been hiding? If I wanted to marry Stephano, I had to come clean. I decided to wait until the next night, when we would exchange our respective surprises.

The restaurant Stephano chose was opulent. I knew this night would be very special indeed. After a lovely dinner and a particularly poignant moment of professed love, Stephano held my hand. He told me he'd been planning a birthday party in my honor a week from now in Portofino. He seemed deeply in love. What better place for him to propose to me than my twenty-first birthday party in Portofino? I made the decision to tell him the truth.

I looked into Stephano's eyes and told him I'd been keeping a secret from him. With the sincerity of a baby puppy, he gazed at me and assured me he wanted to help me with any problem I might have. Any problem of mine, he said, was also his problem.

"Stephano, I haven't told you the truth."

"Yes, my rare jewel, you can tell me anything."

"Are you sure you can handle anything?"

"Darling, I love you. Love is accepting anything your lover says or does and not making value judgments. Tell me, my dear."

"Well, my jewelry—"

"You have *beautiful* jewelry," he interrupted. "Some of the finest I've ever seen."

"Yes, and well, my apartment—"

He interrupted again. "The view is magnificent. You've decorated it impeccably. You are a very talented woman." He squeezed my hand, then added, "For an American, that is."

We both laughed. This was a running joke we had. The French tend to look down on Americans, it is true.

But with all our faults, money seemed to be a great equalizer for Stephano.

"Stephano, please listen. I'm in trouble."

His lighthearted demeanor changed to one of deep concern.

"Tell me what is wrong. How can I help? Oh, darling, talk to me."

"Well, you see, I'm not what I appear to be."

"What do you mean?"

"I am, ah, not a wealthy woman."

Stephano let go of my hand, the one he'd been squeezing and caressing throughout the entire conversation.

"I don't understand," he was gravely concerned.

"Stephano, I'm not rich. As a matter of fact, my clothing and jewels are my only possessions. They were gifts from a wealthy Arab who has been keeping me for months."

"What?" Stephano became indignant.

"Yes. I'm a girl from Beverly Hills who was swept off my feet by a man who brought me here and set me up with the apartment, the car, the furs, the jewels, everything." I had decided that the time wasn't right to reveal that I was a hooker, too.

Stephano's consternation turned to a momentary smile.

"You're kidding, aren't you?"

"No."

"Let me get this straight. You don't own the penthouse apartment?"

"No. But darling, it gets worse."

"How could it get any worse?"

He had a look on his face like the Ex-Lax had just kicked in.

"I have to leave the apartment. My friend is selling it."

Sam's business partner, who didn't like me, had told him that I was hooking in Monte Carlo. I told Sam it wasn't true, but he decided to sell the apartment anyway. I would have to go somewhere else.

After my revelations, Stephano's hand went up in the air, signaling the waiter to bring him the check. For the first time in the months we'd been dating, he gazed at the check with an expression that seemed to say, "What an expensive waste of my time and money! And now this? A check for four champagne cocktails, and the lying bitch had the nerve to order caviar *and* escargot?" Reluctantly, his hand dove into his pocket and retrieved his gold money clip to pay the bill. His mind was anywhere but with me in that restaurant. He draped my sable coat over my shoulders, escorted me to his Mercedes, and deposited me at my soon-to-be-sold penthouse apartment. That was the last I saw of him.

My birthday came and went with no Stephano, no party, and no Portofino. Soon afterward I packed my twelve suitcases, loaded to the brim with the things I'd acquired with Sam's money, and headed back to Los Angeles. Sam soon found another woman to take care of his extramarital needs, and I was back to having to figure out how to support myself.

Some months later, while grabbing a ham and cheese sandwich at the Pink Dot on Sunset Boulevard, I glanced over at a *National Enquirer*. I smiled as I read the headline: "Princess Caroline to wed Stephano Caseraghi!"

LOS ANGELES, SPRING 1984

Val Dumas: They Own You

I was back in Hollywood with no money but lots of expensive clothes. I had been supported by Sam for almost a year. Now that it was over, I hoped I could find another sugar daddy. I found my opportunity at a party in Beverly Hills.

I was having the time of my life at this party, flitting like a butterfly from one handsome, unattached man to the next, when I spotted a very attractive, graying man on the other side of the room. He was Val Dumas, an aging Greek tycoon. He was surrounded by several beautiful young girls. I don't know what possessed me to break the huddle of gorgeous nymphets, but I did. I walked up to him and smiled. I knew I looked good. I guess he thought so too, because within twelve hours I was flying first-class to Las Vegas. To my surprise, he had asked two other young ladies along. This was how I met Liza and Robin.

None of us made love with Val during this trip. We were just his guests, and he wanted us around for luck at the gambling tables. We had a great time spending the money he'd given us for gambling. Each of us had our own suite, compliments of the casino—a testament to the fact that this powerful man was a high roller.

Seventy-two hours later, we were all on a plane back to Los Angeles. I was happy to have made two new friends, Robin and Liza. I liked them both, but Liza was more like me. She also enjoyed life in the fast

lane—good wine, mind-altering drugs, and prostitution when she needed money. We had so much in common that we decided to keep the party going back at
my place with some Quaaludes and hot sex with each
other.

The next day I received a call from Val. He said he
really enjoyed the Vegas trip, and out of the three girls
he had set his sights on me. He wanted to get to know
me better and asked if I would have dinner with him
the following night. I agreed.

When Val picked me up, I was wearing a beautiful
Halston dress purchased on our Las Vegas getaway,
and a push-up bra. I really looked hot. Val whistled his
approval and helped me into his foreign sports car. He
looked great too, and I was just as proud to be with
him as he was to be with me. We headed over to Chi-
nois On Main, one of Wolfgang Puck's restaurants. He
didn't waste any time getting to what was on his
mind.

"You hit it off with Liza, I hear." Val knew everything that went on.

"Did she tell you?"

"Everything," he smiled. "Over dinner, I want to
hear all about what the two of you did together. Every
single detail."

This was fine with me, but I didn't waste any time
telling him what was really on my mind.

"Val, can I ask you something?"

"Anything."

"Would it be possible to borrow some money?"

His look was serious as he studied my face. Then
his eyes slowly traveled down to my breasts. Without
altering his gaze, he put his hand on my thigh. There

was a concerned look on his face. His bushy eyebrows raised as he spoke in a hushed tone.

"Are you having difficulty, darling?"

"Yes. I can't pay my rent."

If he felt he could have, I'm sure he would have shouted, "Yippee!" His controlled joy was that profound. Here he sat, looking into the eyes of a young, beautiful, hard-bodied, and best of all, desperate woman. He patted my thigh gently.

"Honey, I'm here for you. Anything you need. That is, of course, if you're here for me."

"What do you mean?" I knew what he meant, but I wanted to hear the terms. He smiled.

"A beautiful young lady like you shouldn't have to worry her pretty little head over something as insignificant as money. Don't you agree?"

I smiled demurely and nodded.

"What would you say if I took upon myself the burden of paying your rent?"

I was beside myself. That was more than I had hoped for.

"Oh, Val. That would be very generous of you."

"You're old enough to know that nothing comes for free, aren't you?" he asked matter-of-factly.

I nodded again. I knew what was at stake. He was offering to make a major contribution to my peace of mind. It was worth giving an occasional sexual favor, I thought. Then he made his proposed deal.

"Listen, all you have to do is let me visit you once in a while. Do you know what I mean?"

Sure I did. He would pay my rent, and I'd have to subject myself to his tender touch. No problem. I'd had sex for a lot less.

"And another thing," he continued. "I want you to

travel to Las Vegas with me from time to time. You look good at my table. You bring me luck.''

''No problem,'' I said.

I settled into the idea of our upcoming intimate friendship. We were both excited and, like two newly-weds, we toasted with champagne and savored our duck crepes.

Everything went well. I had my own life to live, but it sure did take the pressure off, not having to pay my rent. Once or twice a week Val would come to visit me and I ''earned my keep.'' It wasn't difficult. I actually found him to be quite inoffensive, and his technique improved with my tutelage. But about six months later, at the Desert Inn in Las Vegas, I realized that when someone is paying for you, they own you.

Before going to the Don King Tennis Tournament that weekend, Val insisted we have sex. Since taking care of his sexual needs was my job, it didn't bother me to go down on him and take care of a fantasy or two he'd had earlier that day, on the plane over.

Then we left for the post-tournament party. When I was with Val he demanded that I give him my undivided attention, and I usually complied. But at this event, I was having fun. I knew several of the tennis stars at the party and flirted with a few I didn't know. At the end of the evening, Vitas Gerulaitis and Bjorn Borg, who I happened to know, invited me to another party. Val was gambling, so I agreed to go. When I returned to our suite, however, Val was in a rage.

''Who the hell do you think you are?'' he stormed. ''Do you know who I am?''

''Yes.''

''I'm Val Dumas. I have a reputation here. I didn't

bring you along so you could go off whoring with half the men's tennis team."

"I know Vitas and Bjorn," I said. "We're friends. We were just hotel hopping."

"Don't give me that. I know the kind of hopping you were doing."

"What?"

With that, Val had me thrown out of the hotel. I was escorted to my room by two thugs, where I was instructed to pack my bag. Then I was taken to the front of the hotel and deposited. I stood there for a few moments, embarrassed and stunned. I finally called Bjorn Borg. He felt sorry for me and invited me to sleep on the couch of his suite. I quickly took him up on the offer.

I learned something that night. If someone was paying me for my time, they thought they owned me. It was an expensive lesson. Once again, I found myself in the same situation as thousands other young, beautiful girls in Los Angeles. I had to go back home and worry about how I was going to pay my rent.

SYDNEY, AUSTRALIA, SUMMER 1984

Matt Dillon: Sex In a Sauna

Sometimes a high-priced call girl has a lot of time on her hands, especially when she's on an assignment for an important businessman who only has time for her in the evenings. During these "off-duty" hours things can happen that are entirely unplanned, but very enjoyable.

A very wealthy man named Kerry Packer ordered two California blondes to be flown to Sydney, Australia. He wanted plain, straight sex, and his only requirement was that the girls be beautiful. Madam Alex, the famous Hollywood madam whom I started to work for after Val Dumas abruptly ended our arrangement, thought my girlfriend Paula and I fit the bill. The deal was great—one thousand dollars a day for eleven days in Australia. Air fare, hotel, shopping, meals, everything we could imagine was included.

Sydney, Australia is beautiful in the winter. Because the country is located south of the equator, Australians enjoy the opposite weather from ours. They sun and surf during our winter months and freeze while we enjoy summer. Sydney is very much like San Francisco, a cosmopolitan and international mecca. Though we were world travelers, courtesy of our chosen profession, neither Paula nor I had even been down under and we were looking forward to the trip.

We arrived in Sydney in the early morning. From the moment we stepped off the plane, we were given V.I.P. treatment. A limo took us to the Sabel Townhouse, where Mr. Packer's secretary had arranged everything, including champagne in our room. We were told that Mr. Packer would be seeing each of us that night.

Paula and I were like two little girls in a candy store. The first thing we did was order a meal of fabulous Australian lobster. Next, we went to the swimming pool for some sun and cocktails. The way the men at the pool gawked at us, you'd have thought they'd never seen beautiful women before. We basked in the attention and even decided to take off our string bikini bathing suit tops. Paula was quite lovely. As I looked at her by the pool, I thought about what it would be like to have sex with Paula and Mr. Packer, the three of us. I couldn't imagine Packer or me kicking Paula out of bed.

After a couple of hours of putting suntan lotion on each other and basking by the pool, a bellman came over and told us to call Mr. Packer's secretary. We did.

"Be ready in an hour," she instructed.

Paula and I quickly went up to our rooms, took bubble baths, and prepared for the evening.

A limousine took us to a beautiful high-rise apartment where we would meet this famous Mr. Packer. In fact, he was a very charming gentleman. After dinner we had a brief threesome with him. It turned out that this was to be my only sexual encounter with Mr. Packer on the entire trip, and I still came home with eleven thousand dollars.

For me, the big thrill of the trip occurred at the pool one hot day in the middle of our stay. Wearing only my sun glasses and a bikini bottom that barely covered my pale blonde hair, I noticed a handsome young man staring at me from across the pool. I decided to give the guy a thrill and look his way. As I was performing my slow, sultry move, Paula noticed the thrill-seeker as well.

"Linda, that's Matt Dillon," she said excitedly.

"Get out."

"No, really, Linda. It's Matt Dillon, the actor. I just saw him on television in a rerun of *My Bodyguard*.

"He's awfully cute."

"Only if you like perfection."

We both giggled.

Before long, Matt walked over and sat down on a

lounge chair next to ours. In a slow, southern drawl he said, "Howdy, young ladies. Where are ya'll from?"

"Los Angeles."

"That's where I live," he replied.

"We know who you are," Paula added.

Matt smiled, "You sure are pretty women."

We asked him about the southern accent.

"I'm in character. We're shooting a movie here called *Target* and my character is from the South."

As we chatted, you could almost see the wheels turning in Matt's head, deciding which one of us he wanted. Apparently taking the divide-and-conquer tack, he asked me if I wanted to take a sauna. Trying to keep my cool, I gave a sly smirk to Paula, slowly got up, put on my bikini top and followed his lead.

Matt Dillon didn't have any idea who I was or why I was there. He never asked me one single question. He just walked tall and I followed. Once inside the sauna, he pulled me close to him. We kissed passionately. How many women, I wondered, make love with movie stars just because they get the chance? I was no exception then. It took me about three seconds to decide what to do when he took out his hard rammer: I pulled my bikini bottoms to the side and took a ride. He had a young, firm body and I was more than ready to take him on. The entire time we were pumping, me with my toes pointed skyward, him kneeling on the red-wood slat floor, nobody interrupted us. Maybe you could hear our sounds through the walls. Or maybe we were just lucky.

Thinking back on it now, I don't know how he wouldn't have known I was a whore. I was very, very good at what we were doing. I'd had a lot more practice than most women my age. But he never seemed to suspect it. He didn't use protection, and I wasn't about to ruin the moment to insist upon getting some. When we were done, I walked back to Paula with a smile on my face. I was gloating. After all, Matt had chosen me. Then that son-of-a-bitch Matt started looking at Paula the same way he had just looked at me before we fucked in the sauna!

He asked us both to go out dancing with him that evening. By the end of the night, Matt had taken off with Paula. According to her, he made love with her twice, once that evening and again the next morning. I guess she had something I didn't—she was one up on me.

Neither one of us ever heard from Matt Dillon again. Apparently he thought we were college girls on vacation. Little did he know, if he had to pay for what he got for free, it would have cost him several thousand dollars.

Of all the people I've made love with, movie stars seem to be the most egotistical. And the more famous they are, the less inclined they are to pay for the service. Every once in a while, I think about that time in the sauna in Sydney, and wonder how Matt Dillon would feel had he known he had made love to two prostitutes, on another man's tab.

Dennis Hopper: Sexy Lingerie

*A*ctors who are inclined to pay for sex often don't want straight sex like Matt Dillon did. Actors and other clients who hire prostitutes are more likely to want kinkier stuff such as fetishes or various forms of sadomasochism. Sometimes they are voyeurs. My girlfriend Susan, also a prostitute, had been with Dennis Hopper, famous for his roles in *Easy Rider* and *Blue Velvet*. She knew just what he liked.

I was a bit nervous as I got ready to go with Susan for our gig with Dennis Hopper. I put on my favorite lingerie and packed away some changes into my bag. By the time Susan and I pulled up to his home and got out of her car, however, we both strutted confidently to his front door. Being a professional gives you a sense of confidence that comes in handy when you're meeting new people for the first time.

We rang the doorbell. The door opened, and standing there was Dennis Hopper. The look on his face was like that of a little boy opening a package at Christmas. He greeted Susan as though she were a long-lost friend, hugged her and lifted her up.

"Hi, Susan, you look great. Who's your friend?"

"Her name is Linda. Do you like her?"

"I'm speechless. C'mon in."

He escorted us in and told us to make ourselves comfortable. As he went to get us drinks, Susan looked at me and winked. I was awestruck by the beautiful furniture and art on display. When Dennis returned,

Susan commented on some of the masterpieces adorning the white walls. He talked to her, but his gaze kept drifting to my body, as if he were undressing me mentally. I knew he wouldn't be disappointed when he saw the real thing.

Once the small talk was over, Dennis asked coyly, "What did you bring to wear?"

Susan reached into her bag and took out a blue lace bodysuit.

Dennis nodded his approval. "Got anything else?" Dennis looked over at me as Susan rifled through her bag.

"I'm wearing mine already," I said. "Shall I take off my dress?"

"Be my guest."

I stood up, looked him directly in the eyes and slowly began lifting my dress, first past my thighs, revealing my beautiful long legs, then slowly up past my hips. I was wearing a white satin-and-lace garter belt, bra, panty, and stocking ensemble. He took in each piece as my dress languidly made its way up above my head, past my shoulders and long hair. I shook out my hair as I dropped the dress over a chair. I stood proudly in my high heels, with my legs spread, posing for him. He was mesmerized.

I gazed deeply into his eyes while stared back, mouth agape. He looked euphoric.

"Is this something that appeals to you?" I asked.

As Dennis nodded his head up and down, I swear I noticed a slight drool.

Not to be outdone, Susan piped in, "Dennis, how about this?" Dennis reluctantly turned to Susan, who was holding up a black lace bustier and panties.

"Nice . . . real nice."

His eyes went back to me.

"Or this?" Susan was frustrated. She pulled out some fancy lace panties, a garter belt, and stockings, but she couldn't get his attention. He just nodded, unable to take his eyes off my body.

Susan shrugged, went into his bathroom, and came out moments later wearing her high heels and lingerie.

Dennis put on some music and Susan and I paraded in front of him, walking back and forth, taking turns teasing him and dancing to the beat. At some point during the procession, we each took off our bras. I took an ice cube from my drink and held it against my nipples, one at a time. Photographers do this to models to make their nipples hard. I offered the cube to Susan, but she declined.

We were both strutting around, wearing only garter belts, stockings, and smiles. Susan gyrated to the beat of Bob Seger and the Silver Bullet Band while I prepared the sex toys.

As Dennis watched, Susan and I made what appeared to be mad, passionate love to each other. I kissed her lips, stroked her hair, her breasts, her thighs, and lingered on her pussy. We ooh'd and aah'd our way to a frenzied pitch and then, after glancing at a watch on my wrist and noticing his time was up, I gave Susan a subtle signal. We each gave our incredible squeals, as though we had just had the best sex of our lives. Dennis never touched us. He only liked to watch.

We packed up to head out the door, each of us clutching $250 in crisp, green bills. Not bad for one hour's work. As my fanny passed by his gaze, Dennis asked us if we wanted to join him for lunch at a trendy restaurant off of Main Street in Santa Monica. We were flattered that he invited us. We were also very hungry.

"Sure, Dennis. We're game."

"We'll be joined by a producer friend of mine. I'm sure you won't mention what just went on," he said, smiling.

The restaurant was one of my favorites, featuring delicious California cuisine. As we drank red wine and ate warm duck salad, various fans came by and asked for Dennis Hopper's autograph. I must admit, it was a bit of a rush knowing that none of them would ever suspect what we had all just been doing together. When his producer friend joined us, Dennis introduced us to him as old friends.

At the end of our lunch, we kissed each other lightly, cheek to cheek, and said good bye. Dennis must have liked our show, because he paid for a repeat performance some time later—but sadly, it didn't include lunch.

DALLAS, TEXAS, FALL 1987

Saudi Prince: Dates a Soap Star

*P*rostitutes have to be pretty good actresses. They must pretend to actually care about their trick. They often have to serve as therapists, surrogate mothers, wives, or lovers. Some of my performances have warranted at least an Emmy nomination— particularly the time Madam Alex wanted me to play the role of a soap opera star. I was so convincing, I almost believed it myself.

It started in Madam Alex's Beverly Hills apartment. She later told me about the conversation she had with my client, a wealthy Saudi prince.

"What's your pleasure today, Mohammed?" Her voice was mature and deep, but unmistakably feminine.

"I want an American soap opera star."

"I can get whatever you want. Do you prefer blonde or brunette?" Madam Alex knew she couldn't get her hands on a real life soap star. She did, however, know someone who was a good enough actress to pull the job off.

"Blonde. Absolutely."

"Blue eyes?"

"Whatever. Just make sure she's blonde and works on an American television soap opera. My wife would kill me if she knew. She's addicted to these things. But what the hell, that's what makes it exciting, knowing my wife is probably a fan of the young lady. As I shall be as well, once I've had sex with her."

"I have just the girl. She's beautiful, blonde, with long legs, and class up the wazoo."

"Good. How much?"

"How long do you need her?"

"One evening. Dinner with business associates, then a nightcap. And maybe a little something in the morning to get my day started right."

Madam Alex had filled thousands of orders like this before—everything from young women who dressed up as prepubescent Girl Scouts and banged on the door selling cookies, to boys who look like girls, to the man who wanted an Elvira, Mistress of the Night clone. A soap opera star was something new to her, but it was easily within the realm of possibility. She was leafing through her black address book looking for my name as she concluded the conversation.

"That will cost you six thousand dollars, plus transportation."

The Saudi prince agreed and plans were made.

When Madam Alex called me on the phone, I knew something special was about to be offered. She had a smile in her voice.

"Hello, Linda?"

"Hi, Alex."

"I've got a special assignment for you."

"Not the sadist in Palm Springs, I hope."

"Not him. I have a Saudi prince in Dallas. He wants a soap opera star. I thought of you right away."

"Me? I'm flattered."

"Sure. You can pull it off. You've got the diction, the Newport Beach breeding. You're a natural."

"I studied acting, you know."

"I know. That's why I'm calling you."

"When is the date?"

"You'll take a plane to Dallas tomorrow afternoon. A limo driver will meet you, and you will be escorted to his hotel. First class. This one should be fun. When you're through, who knows, you may want to get back into acting and audition for a real soap."

We both laughed and said good-bye. This was an assignment I knew I could sink my teeth into.

When I landed in Dallas, wearing a blue cashmere blazer with a tweed mini skirt and pale beige silk blouse, a young, handsome man approached me. At first I thought he was the limo driver, but he turned out to be my john, the Saudi prince. I thought to myself, this is going to be easier than I thought. I wouldn't have to act with him. We picked up my baggage, and once outside he handed them to his driver. We entered the stretch limo, and in a very professional manner my prince gave me my evening's instructions.

"I've got some work to do before dinner. My penthouse suite has several rooms. Choose one and make yourself comfortable. Be ready for dinner at eight o'clock."

The hotel was beautiful—glass elevators, flowers in planters along the railings. We rode up to the top floor. The suite had a marble entrance and looked like something out of a James Bond movie. It had elegant furnishings and paintings with a contemporary flair.

In no time I had a bubble bath running. As I luxuriated in the fragrant foamy water, my mind drifted to another Arabian man, my first paying job, Adnan Khashoggi. I had come a long way since those innocent days.

I put on a black organza and satin minidress that covered just the right places and exposed the others. I was a perfect combination of tasteful and tasty. This client's business associates would surely be wishing they had the pleasure of a soap star like me for the evening, just like their fortunate host.

At the designated time, I walked into the living room. The prince gasped. He was wearing a Zegna suit and Bijan fragrance for men. With my dress, black stockings, and Boucheron perfume, we looked like the perfect couple.

When we arrived at the restaurant, the maitrê d' behaved as if he was greeting the President of the United States. I'm sure his palm had been greased generously in preparation for this moment. The prince was a man who definitely thought ahead.

We were escorted to our table. There, already

seated, were four well-dressed men ranging in age from early forties to mid-sixties. Their eight eyebrows collectively raised as I stood before them. The prince introduced me and each man gently shook my hand. One man, I'll call him Harry, lingered with a seductive grip. It was embarrassing for the prince, but he chose to ignore the gesture.

The evening seemed to be going well. Every man was impressed with "who I was." All of their wives, it seems, were addicted to the soaps. I laid it on thick. I fabricated stories about how I was discovered and how long I'd been going to cattle calls before my big break. I talked about my agent, my manager, my business manager, and my attorney, and I lamented at the small percentage that was left over for me after they all took their cut. The only hitch came when, after telling them I worked on "All My Children," one of them commented on the fact that I lived on the opposite coast from where they shoot that show. I picked up the slip like a pro.

"I fly for the shoot and come home on the weekends."

"You must get tired of traveling," one of the men queried.

The prince jumped in, "Lucky for me, she still has time to visit."

"Do you go to Saudi Arabia just for the prince?" Harry asked.

"Of course. I'd go anywhere to see Mohammed." I turned to him and smiled. "You know that."

"You're a lucky man," Harry was looking into my eyes as he spoke.

The prince picked up on this and changed the subject. "So tell me, Linda, what is your character doing over the next couple of weeks?"

"I'll never tell. I'm sworn to secrecy." I lied, of course. I didn't know.

"You can tell us," Harry chided.

"You wouldn't want me to lose my job, would you?" I said, sweetly.

"Of course not," the prince chimed in. "Let's ask Linda questions she can answer." Saved by the bell. "So, Linda, who is your love interest on the show at the moment?"

"It's, uh, Chad this week!" At this point, I didn't even know if there was a character named Chad. Luckily, I would be on the plane before the airing of the next episode of "All My Children."

By the end of the evening, I'd managed to win the heart of all four guests, including my host. He was very proud to have brought along a "girlfriend" of such lauded Hollywood stature. As I was leaving, Harry discreetly slipped me his card. But I had had enough of the charade. I didn't want to think about continuing it at some later point with Harry. Toward the end of the evening, I had an aching feeling in the pit of my stomach, wishing I could really have been the successful actress I was pretending to be. It felt so good to have the respect and admiration of these successful men. They all treated me like I was someone special. If they only knew that they were really talking to a high-priced hooker from Beverly Hills, with a cocaine habit and a madam. Sure I was an actress, but not the kind they thought I was. My acting took place in a bedroom or an expensive hotel suite.

The prince said good-night to his guests and we were whisked off to his hotel in the limo. There, the prince took off my clothes, and then his own. Like an old "Lawrence Welk Show" rerun, it was over in the time it took for Mr. Welk to say, "And-a one, and-a two". The champagne bubbles didn't even have a chance to pop before he was thanking me for my time and making arrangements for when he wanted me in the morning.

The morning brought "And-a three and-a four," and that was that. Before I knew it, I was on a flight back to Los Angeles. As I stared out at the blue sky and white clouds, my mind drifted to the Marilyn Monroe movie, *The Prince and the Showgirl*. Only in my story, I didn't get the guy. I never do.

COLDWATER CANYON, SPRING 1988

Don Henley: A Three-Woman Man

*R*ock stars apparently have a hard time satisfying the sexual appetites they acquire when they are on the road. When they are on hiatus from touring or their season in the limelight is over, they still need their fix. They long for the good old days of young groupies throwing keys, phone numbers, and panties onto the stage after a wild performance.

When I was working for Madam Alex in Beverly Hills, some of her regular customers had voracious appetites for sex. They hired girls in multiples—twos, threes, and more. Some of us got to know each other and what to expect. It wasn't always fun.

One night I got a telephone call from my girlfriend, Pam.

"Hi, Linda. I need another girl for Don Henley."

"Not tonight, please. I'm tired."

"Linda, I don't ask many favors. Madam Alex needs three girls. I've only got two, and I'm one of them."

"Can't you call someone else?" I really was tired.

There was a pleading tone in her voice, "Please? I'll owe you one."

Pam usually never resorted to pleading. I knew exactly what I was in for; I'd been with Don before. And I knew why she was so desperate. If she promised three girls and showed up with only two, it might be her last gig with this icon of the baby boomer set. And he was a good-paying regular. I decided I'd help her out.

An hour later, Pam's Mercedes pulled up to the front of my apartment building. She called me from her phone to let me know she'd arrived. I grabbed my bag of sexy underwear, prophylactics, and sex toys, and headed downstairs. On the drive up to Don's house, we made small talk. For a seasoned pro like I was, tonight was routine.

The third girl was waiting for us in front of Don Henley's home. Very matter-of-factly, the three of us strolled up to the front entrance. Pam rang the bell. As soon as Don opened the door, we knew we were "on"—our act kicked into gear. Suddenly, we were like three girls from Cyndi Lauper's music video, "Girls Just Want to Have Fun." We smiled, laughed, and acted like we were having the best time in the world. Don gave us drinks. Within fifteen minutes we were all parading around in sexy underwear and talking dirty as we began to undress him. We knew exactly what we were expected to do.

"Bend over, all three of you. Over here on the couch," he ordered.

We obeyed. We all lined up in a row and we gave great reaction performances as he swung his bat into each and every one of us, one after another, after another. A few strokes with me and he was out. Within a moment or two, Pam was up at the plate and he was giving her a long drive to left field. After several more swings, Don was on to the third girl. From one to another to another, over and over and over. Among the three of us women, there were times when our eyes met. We exchanged looks of resolve, each silently hoping (against judgment born of experience) that the evening would not last too long. This, however, was not to be.

We were next directed into the bedroom, where he proceeded to take us on again, one after another. He was tireless. Pam and I would just as soon have been painting our nails or reading a book, but you could never tell by our reactions.

"Oh Don, you're the king."

"Take me baby, it feels so good."

"Check me into the Hotel California, sweet thing."

No doubt about it, we were pros.

After several hours, Don finally nodded off, exhausted. As usual, we had been paid up front. So, careful not to wake him (I'd made that mistake one previous evening, and lived to regret it when I was stuck there for another two hours), Pam and I quickly dressed and made our exit. We said good-bye to "girl number three," and Pam drove me home, each about a thousand dollars richer. Don is married now, to a beautiful young lady. Though I normally might feel a twinge of jealousy at anyone finding marital bliss, in this case she can have him.

A Madam Waiting to Happen

*L*ittle has been written about Heidi Fleiss, her history, and the circumstances that propelled her into becoming a madam. What I have to say about Heidi is from the perspective of a friend who knew her before, during, and after the events that changed her life—and her father's—forever.

Heidi was not a typical prostitute. She didn't come to Hollywood with stars in her eyes, dreaming of becoming a famous actress. Nor was she the victim of a drug-pushing pimp, turned out to do tricks under a street lamp in a seedy part of Hollywood. Heidi was born with that famous, cocky, arrogant smile, the daughter of a successful physician and doting mother. She was raised to appreciate and expect the finer things in life. But if there was ever a quirk in her personality that drove her into "the life," in my opinion it was her obsession with older men.

She seemed to be searching in vain for a man who would be as nurturing and supportive as her father. Slender, coquettish, provocative Heidi went from one Dorian Gray to another. But instead of finding men who would nurture her business talents, she vainly attempted to get the support she craved from men who used and abused her.

Heidi's first big crush was on a man named Paul F., an overweight, middle-aged womanizer. At the time she met Paul, Heidi was an innocent, misguided waiflike girl, sheltered by her father from the task of having to support herself. Prostitution was completely foreign to her consciousness. Heidi fell for Paul, but the trouble with their May/September romance was that Paul couldn't keep his hands off any and every other sweet young thing he could manage to seduce.

Paul's lust for exploring the unknown hurt Heidi deeply. With each indiscretion, Heidi became more and more determined to win Paul back. With undying devotion and loyalty, she tried to elicit his love. Like many young women frustrated by her inability to change a man's wanton ways, Heidi took out her disillusion and disappointment at the dinner table. After a time, she began to gain weight. With each pound she put on, she became more depressed. Her depression didn't lift until she met another ancient, a Yoda-like Svengali named Bernie Kornfeld. Heidi flipped over Bernie.

Bernie owned a famous mansion in Beverly Hills called Greyhall. At one time he was a big deal-maker in finance. His luck ran out when, according to him, his partner screwed him. In any event, he went from original, priceless art to reproductions, and from having castles in Europe and flats in London to only one mansion in Coldwater Canyon.

Bernie was known for giving shelter to at least a half-dozen nymphets at a time, innocent young ladies in need of a place to stay. The total number of "Kornfeld shelterees" over the years has to be into the hundreds. The girls would parade around his house in outfits ranging from "fanny panties," to sexy, revealing lingerie, to spandex bodysuits. And at times there firm-breasted, lithe beauties would unabashedly parade around the mansion in the nude.

Heidi somehow managed to put up with all this. Bernie was otherwise a lovable guy; he never drank, never smoked, and never did drugs. If the beautiful young ladies who lived at his estate did these things, he simply turned his head the other way. He let the girls to pretty much what they wanted. All he expected was to enjoy the view and, if the girl was right, partake of her bounty once in a while.

Besides women, Bernie loved cars. His driveway was lined with beautiful automobiles that would be the envy of any serious collector. The young girls at the house felt free to ask him for the keys to any car that struck their fancy. The girls would often tool around Sunset Strip, the Beverly Center, or Rodeo Drive, usually oblivious to the value or rarity of the cars they were driving.

Bernie sometimes even gave cars to his favorite paramours. He bought a classic Mustang convertible for Heidi when she was his main squeeze. But despite his generosity, and much to Heidi's dismay, there were always other girls in Bernie's life. He just couldn't keep his hands off them. I first met Heidi as she was breaking up with Bernie and starting to date another womanizer, film director Ivan Nagy.

At that time Heidi had a real estate license. She enjoyed being around beautiful homes in Beverly Hills, Brentwood, and Bel Air. She fit in. Heidi had breeding, and she was never afraid of hard work.

She lived then in Beverly Hills on Doheny Drive, at the apartment of Jennifer Young, the daughter of Heidi's boss, realtor Elaine Young. Jennifer's father was the famed actor Gig Young. Jennifer's apartment was only blocks away from Madam Alex, but this was before Heidi knew the famous Beverly Hills madam.

I met Heidi at a party at Ivan Nagy's house. I remember when she entered the room: her confidence was infectious. She had the self-assurance of Madonna as she plopped onto the down-filled brocade couch as if she owned the place. I looked over at this seemingly innocent, brown-eyed girl, and she looked back at me. After an awkward moment of silence, she said something I will never forget,

"I love you."

"What?" I was surprised at not only her words, but the sincerity with which she spoke them.

"I love you," she repeated. She sat close to me and seemed to be staring right into my soul. It was quite obvious that she was at least bisexual. It felt good. I've always been attracted to women who like women. From that moment on we became good friends.

Sometime after we met, Heidi suggested that I move into Bernie Kornfield's home. I didn't know she was still in love with him. By then, she was already involved with Ivan Nagy. Heidi set everything up for me—something she was good at. I stood by as she picked up the phone and called Bernie.

"Hello, Bernie? It's Heidi. A friend of mine, her name is Linda, has been staying with me for a few weeks and I was hoping you might have room for her at your place."

As Bernie responded, Heidi looked over at me and winked.

"Bernie, thanks. By the way, she's beautiful and a lot of fun."

She hung up the phone and gave me Bernie's address.

When I arrived by taxi at the mansion in Coldwater Canyon, Bernie greeted me at the door. He took me up to someone's room and told the young woman living there that she had to move to another room, one without a private bathroom. I was embarrassed, but apparently upon seeing me he decided to give me the best guest bedroom in the house. As the girl packed, Bernie showed me the view over the pool. "This is my finest guest room, for my beautiful new guest" he said proudly.

The house was filled with gorgeous young girls, most of them anxious to give Mr. Kornfield sex any time he wanted. I, too, was willing. After all, I thought, he had been kind to me and he let me stay in his mansion. When I agreed to give someone sex it didn't mean I was involved with them emotionally, but Heidi didn't understand that. One day Bernie asked me to accompany him to the Bahamas, and he asked Heidi to join us. She declined and abruptly stopped talking to me. I was upset and went to Heidi's apartment to ask her what was wrong.

"Heidi, is it that Bernie asked me to go to the Bahamas?"

"Of course not. Why would that bother me?" I didn't know if she was being sarcastic or not. I chose to believe the latter.

"Good. I've been all over the world, but never to the Bahamas."

"Sounds like fun." She added, "I might join you if I can get free."

When the time came to take the trip, Heidi didn't show. Bernie and I had a fabulous time. We had lots of good food, great wine, laughs, and sex. To me, the sex was just sport fucking. I had no emotional involvement, only honest gratitude to a guy who treated me well. I had fucked guys for a lot less. But I still felt guilty about Heidi. I called Beverly Hills to see what had happened to her, and she hung up the phone on me.

I later learned that Heidi was very angry that Bernie had asked me on the trip. She was even more upset that I had accepted. Apparently, she was still in love with him. It took a long time for her to forgive me, but she eventually did.

Little did she know then that her problems were just beginning.

Ivan Nagy:
The Man Who Made the Madam

*W*hen Heidi finally reached her saturation point with Bernie Kornfeld, those of us who considered her a friend breathed a sigh of relief. We thought she'd finally seen the light. But it wasn't long before Heidi had fallen for Ivan Nagy, another older, arrogant womanizer, who would prove to be far more destructive than any of Heidi's former boyfriends. Nagy played to Heidi's unrelenting desire to please a man. As undeserving as the others were, this man was really bad news. He proceeded to move into Heidi's life and take over.

A former photographer and ex-professional hockey

player, Ivan was known for taking girls out on his sixty-foot boat and expecting sex in return. He categorized girls as either models or hookers. He told both Heidi and me that we weren't pretty enough to be models, so we might as well be hookers. When Heidi complied, it broke my heart. I felt like it was okay for me to prostitute. I knew the score, I'd been around. But Heidi seemed so naive, innocent, and eager to please. Ivan took advantage of her main weakness, her "daddy" thing.

Just like a pimp, Ivan wasn't jealous of the men Heidi had sex with for money. He encouraged Heidi to get into the "business" so she could get funds for clothes to wear when she sold real estate. She also needed cash for something else—her high gambling debts. Heidi loves to gamble.

For a while, everything seemed to be going great for Heidi. She worked at real estate, hoping for some good sales, and on the side she was a part-time prostitute. All of Heidi's men were provided by her neighbor, Madam Alex, whom she met through Nagy. Heidi and I often spent time with the same clients. She had a couple of regular customers. One was a man from Texas who owned television stations. The other was a very sick man who enjoyed having girls brought out to Palm Springs to participate in perverted sexual games.

Even with her regulars, Heidi was still pretty much a part-time hooker. Her big leap to full-time Madam came through a series of events that could have been right out of a Sidney Sheldon novel. It had the makings of a good miniseries, rife with intrigue, arrests, burglary, and her dear old boyfriend, Ivan Nagy.

Madame Alex had just been busted for the umpteenth time. It was a miracle that I was spared from arrest that time. I showed up at her Beverly Hills apartment just after everyone had been taken to the station. The police were packing up and heading out. Somehow I managed to convince them that I was just someone who was stopping by and had nothing to do with her business. Maybe it was the way I looked pleadingly into the eyes of a Vice Detective. Who knows? They let me go on my way.

During this period, Heidi's value to Madam Alex increased to monumental proportions. While Madam Alex was dealing with her legal problems, Heidi became her go-between and confidante, enabling at least some of Madam Alex's operations to continue. Madam Alex knew her phone was being tapped and referred all calls to Heidi, who fielded customers like a trooper. Heidi discovered to her surprise that she had a talent for body brokering. Ivan Nagy, in his typically abusive way, told Heidi she would be lucky to become a madam.

"After all," he told her, "you're not beautiful. You're not what California clients want. They're looking for blonde-haired, long-legged, sexy, innocent-looking girls." Ivan convinced Heidi that she was fortunate to be given such a golden opportunity. He continued to beat her down: "Heidi, you're great on the phone, but you'll never be a high-class call girl. Not with your looks. Let's face it, you're too ugly to make it as a hooker!"

Meanwhile, Ivan planned his move. During her down time due to jail and legal hearings, Madame Alex's valuable client list was given to Heidi, who appropriated it. It was Ivan's brainchild for Heidi to take over for Madam Alex. Heidi was in it for the fun, excitement, and some say, the money. But Ivan—boyfriend co-conspirator—engineered the maneuver.

Sometimes I wonder why Ivan walked away without so much as a slap on the wrist, while Heidi was left with a prison sentence, fines, and an IRS problem that almost rivals that of Leona Helmsley. Both women have been hoisted up to the slaughtering block and, like the whores of Babylon, sacrificed as examples for all to see. The johns and the behind-the-scenes pimp, Nagy, all got off scot-free. In my opinion, as one who was there, Heidi was not the person—or not the only person—who should have been sent to jail.

PALM SPRINGS, WINTER 1989

Mr. Sick F. Beating in the Desert

I discovered two truths a long time ago: money can buy practically anything, and there are a lot of sick people out there with a lot of money.

During her Madam Alex days, Heidi Fleiss had one regular customer who was heavily into sado-masochism. I'll call this baboon Mr. Sick F.

The first time Heidi told me about Sick F. and the money he pays for girls, my mind went reeling. For three days with Sick F., I would come home with between ten and twenty thousand dollars. I told her I wouldn't mind making that kind of money. After learning I would get the assignment, I had fantasies about all the things I would buy with what I was about to earn. My daydreaming continued until the limo pulled up to the strikingly ornate, white-stone pillared entrance of the exclusive hotel in Rancho Mirage. I was greeted with the attention usually afforded a foreign dignitary. The hotel management considered Mr. Sick F. an excellent customer, and I'm sure he was. What he did behind the walls of his stately bungalow was apparently of no concern to them. In the hotel business, the management often plays "See no evil, hear no evil." Mr. Sick F. paid his large hotel bills with an American Express Platinum card and that's all that seemed to matter. Occasionally, a hotel employee would pass by the remote bungalow in the night, and be shocked to hear muffled screams behind closed doors. Otherwise, it was hotel business as usual.

It was customary for Sick F. to have young ladies arrive in pairs. However, my partner-to-be, a dominatrix, had already been with him for a day before I arrived. Because of Heidi's briefing I knew what to expect on the monetary end, and I had been in the business long enough to suspect the money would not come easily. But I was completely unprepared for the extreme pain, humiliation, and degradation I was about to attempt to endure.

When I was introduced to Mr. Sick F., I studied the man before me. He was small in stature, but had the assertiveness of a CEO of a Fortune 500 company. He looked me over, then spoke.

"Tell me you name."

"Linda." I thought about using another name so he couldn't find me at a later date, but decided to tell him the truth. The real truth was that I was scared. Since accepting the assignment, I'd heard rumors— very bad rumors.

"Linda, I'd like you to meet Sunday." Mr. Sick F.

pointed to another girl in the room. She was beautiful. Short red hair, green eyes, and four-inch stiletto heels that supported the longest legs I'd ever seen. She stood with one hip jutting out.

"Hello." I looked into her eyes. Though she was wearing a black rubber bodysuit, her voice was gentle and soft, unlike her ominous appearance.

Mr. Sick F. continued, "Sunday will be disciplining you over the next few days. She's skilled at delivering pain and the most severe forms of punishment."

Sunday smiled. Mr. Sick F. went on, "You know you've been bad, don't you? You slut! You're so ugly, you don't even deserve to be here. I told Heidi to send someone beautiful. Look at you, you whore. You shouldn't be allowed to be in the presence of Sunday or myself. A slave like you deserves to be beaten."

It was a mind game. I knew it. I'd been told I was beautiful from my earliest recollection, at the age of five. And since that time I'd been told by more men than I could remember. Mr. Sick F. was just playing a degradation game. He excused himself and went to the bathroom.

Sunday walked over to me, gazed into my eyes, then whispered into my ear, "Don't worry, Linda, I won't hurt you too badly. I'll try to go easy on you." I felt relief, if only for a moment.

When Mr. Sick F. returned, he began to give detailed instructions to Sunday. He let her know, in no uncertain terms, how he expected my punishment to be delivered. Then it started. As she worked me over physically, he worked on me psychologically. For the first time in my life I could understand how people could be beaten to the point where their spirit is broken and they willingly become slaves.

The entire experience was not unlike the scenes in the movie *Pulp Fiction*, where a submissive slave is kept chained in a small box. Wearing a black leather body-suit and head mask with metal zippers strategically located over the mouth and other bodily openings, the slave was held captive by two rednecks. Occasionally these men would bring him out and take turns beating and raping him. From my desert experience with Sick F., I realized these things happen every day.

After hours of emotional and physical torture—there was no need to pretend I was in pain, it was all to real—we finally took a break for something to eat. I was weak, exhausted, and hurting. Mr. Sick F. insisted that Sunday and I enter the dining room wearing summer beach cover-ups with slits up the side and no underwear. My beaten buns were exposed at the back, along with a hint of my barely exposed pussy. There was a small red spot on the upper front of my dress, the result of a bleeding nipple, raw from the nipple clips placed there by Sunday. Mr. Sick F. insisted they remain in place and not be removed for dinner. After a moment of embarrassment, the maitrê d' delicately informed us that there was a dress code.

"Mr. Sick F., I'm sure you can appreciate the fact that we have a dress code. The girls are lovely, don't get me wrong, but I believe our patrons may find their attire a bit distracting, to say the least."

At this point, a strange thing happened to me. I could feel myself beginning to lose my will. I knew that if I didn't do something about getting out of there, I might lose it entirely. When Mr. Sick F. got up to go to the bathroom I asked Sunday, "How long have you known him?"

"A couple of years."

"You've been doing this for a couple of years?" I couldn't believe it.

"Sure. I started out in your position and eventually worked my way up to dominatrix."

"How many girls have you worked with?"

"Dozens."

"Doesn't it have a permanent effect on their psyche?"

"Maybe. But the money's good."

She seemed pleased with herself, and went on to brag, "I'm picking up my custom Harley Davidson next week."

"You make a lot of money?"

"Sure. I bought my own house from this client alone."

"Your own a house?" All I could think of was how much she'd been through to have made enough to purchase her own home.

"If you play your cards right, Linda, you can make a lot of money. Let me give you a tip; scream more. He likes that."

"You told me you'd be taking it easy on me."

"Honey, I have. He likes it much rougher. But I figured, you're new. I have to break you in."

"Sunday, I can't take this. It isn't worth any amount of money."

Sunday saw Mr. Sick F. approaching.

"Shhhh! Here he comes." She continued in a whisper, "You're giving up a good john, honey. Take if from me, it gets easier and easier."

She was wrong. Before long, I'd had more than enough. Luckily, I was paid daily. So when the time was right, with three thousand dollars in my pocket, I split back to L.A. I was as broken a woman as I'd ever been.

As a repeat "object of his affection," I don't know how Heidi stood the abuse from this man. Every time Heidi told me she was going out to Palm Springs to see Mr. Sick F., I felt sorry for her. I also felt bad for the younger girls who were regularly sent this client's way. They were in for a sadistic experience far greater than that administered by the most base of pimps, sociopaths, and sickos.

I thank my lucky stars I'm not in the business anymore and do not have to associate with men like Mr. Sick F. People with fetishes get sicker and sicker. As time goes by, the sadistic acts they need to get their kicks only escalate.

LOS ANGELES, 1990's

James Caan: A Privileged Few

The first time I met actor James Caan was quite a while ago, before I was a hooker. Ronnie Caan, James' brother, invited a girlfriend of mine to a party at the Westwood Marquis Hotel. This girlfriend asked me to come long. The Westwood Marquis is a beautiful extremely elegant hotel as well as a big-time industry hang out. The number of show biz events held there almost equals the number of executives who check into rooms and grab an afternoon screening of a new secretary or starlet from the studio. It's quite a popular place.

I was about nineteen then, and men were always after me. It felt good to be desired. As I reached for an hors d'oeuvre, I looked up to see James Caan about three inches away, grinning his famous half smirk, half smile. I recognized him immediately, and I smiled back. I was very young when *The Godfather* movies came out, but like millions of moviegoers I was still taken by James Caan's charm. It seemed like a fantasy come true when I became the object of this macho man's attention. In less than five minutes he was holding both of my hands and looking into my eyes. Then he did that quick double take of his, where he looks away as if to see if anyone can hear.

"Let's get out of this dump," he said. "You're too beautiful to be wasted on the masses."

With that, I waved good-bye to my girlfriend and headed out the door for points unknown.

James Caan has a quality that, from my personal experience of men in Hollywood, is not entirely unique: he loves sex. Actually, it's more like he's obsessed with sex, but not intercourse. He's crazy about licking pussy.

Before I knew what hit me, I was alone with him in a hotel room sans my panties and, for lack of a better way to describe it, squatting on his face. The man went on for hours and hours. He just couldn't seem to get enough. There were times when I had to stand up, due to severe cramping in my calves. As I did this, he'd reach up for me and pull me down to my "birthing" position, oblivious of my need for medical attention.

My second "date" with Caan took place at Hugh Hefner's Playboy Mansion. He attended the function alone, and the minute he spotted me he grabbed my hand and led me into an unoccupied bedroom. After a few drinks from the bottle he brought along, he told me to "assume the position," the one I knew all too well. Moments later there I was again, exhausted, legs cramping, looking down on this man who was drooling as he lapped me up.

I honestly don't know how he was able to breathe. He never came up for air. At one point I thought about placing a snorkel in the side of his mouth, or one of those tubes that clip under the nose and attach to an oxygen tank, just to make sure he didn't suffocate. For what seemed like forever, I remained in my deep-knee-bend position, taking it like the groupie that I then was. What I found to be totally strange about James Caan was the fact that he never once asked me to lick him.

I was grateful at that tender age for the opportunity to serve such a talented actor for free, even though my rent was due, my telephone was about to be turned off, and I didn't know if I'd have money for gas the next day. Usually high on drugs or alcohol, I enjoyed the "attention" James gave me over the years. I realize now that my only value to him was an object for his obsession. He never gave me a gift or took me out to dinner in all the years he knew me. But this is the way it goes in Hollywood. There is straight sex, bi-sex, sex for pay, mercy sex, sick sex, and for many actors, star sex.

Linda

Glenn Frey: Simply the Best

*M*adam Alex often sent me on assignments with famous people. This was routine and part of the job. After a while, the names and faces seemed to meld together, the only thing I remember about the men were how much money they gave in tips. Of all of the johns I've been with, the only one who was memorable or who I would have done for free was musician Glenn Frey, formerly of the Eagles.

On this assignment I was wearing a short green silk dress and a modest amount of makeup. Madam Alex liked me to dress in a simple, elegant, and provocative style that reflected my Newport Beach breeding. I rang the doorbell and he answered.

"Linda, come in," Glenn said, smiling. He was obviously pleased with what he saw, and Glenn looked beautiful to me as well. It was clear that he took good care of himself. There was a quiet confidence about him; he wasn't flashy or arrogant, like some rock stars I'd been with, or drugged up and strung out, like many others. He was very respectful.

For a prostitute, having sex is usually as matter-of-fact as washing your face. And as a rule, I'm very professional. I had learned not to get emotionally involved with a john. But tonight was different for some reason. I was so nervous, I was almost shaking. My heart took over and I got lost in the desire to believe this man really cared about me, that I wasn't a hooker

194

for hire but a girlfriend who'd come to spend a relaxing evening with my handsome, sensitive paramour.

The evening began like a date. Glenn asked questions about my life and my childhood. We didn't talk money—that had been taken care of by Madam Alex. And though I knew that my part of the evening's take would be five hundred dollars, this time I wasn't passing my time thinking about how I would spend the money.

After a while, we started kissing, like high school sweethearts. Electricity shot through my body when his tongue lightly touched mine. My heartbeat matched his. "Linda, would you like to come to my bedroom?"

"Yes." What a shock. No john ever asks.

He lifted me up in his arms, and I felt like Scarlet O'Hara in *Gone with the Wind*.

"I want to be gentle," he said, as he lay my body down on his king-sized bed. I was lost in the moment as he slowly slipped my silk dress above my head. My blonde hair cascaded onto the pillow. He licked my neck and his tonge began to lightly caress my nipples. His mouth and tongue moved to my navel as he continued to gently lick and suck on the skin of my flat stomach. I took a deep breath, hoping he'd make his way down between my thighs. He took his time, but eventually he got there. His fingers spread me wide open and his tongue did a dance inside of me.

Our lovemaking lasted all night. We'd work each other up and down with little rest in between, then melded together again, each feeling more comfortable inside one another than apart. I now understand how this man was capable of writing the song "All Night Lover." In it, Glenn describes how he knows the women will be back for more because there's nothing like an all–night lover.

I later stopped by Madam Alex's apartment and collected my fee. Apparently Glenn enjoyed the evening, because he requested me an additional four times over the next several months. These were "command performances" of the highest caliber.

But I made the mistake of getting emotionally involved. I fell in love. I wanted him to be my boyfriend. Each time we said good-bye, he gently kissed my lips and I was left with a reality often experienced by prostitutes—I was for hire and he was only a john.

To this day, when I think back to my experiences with Glenn, I can't help fantasizing about what might have been had we met under normal circumstances. A real sadness comes over me. Given where I am today and where I've been, it's bittersweet to daydream about living a normal life with a husband and children. As a young girl, that normal life was something I always expected I would have. But it's something I've never known yet, and now may never know.

CENTURY CITY, 1990

Oscar: Sex Under the Desk

*M*ost hookers have their regular clients. Depending on the price a call girl charges and the places she frequents, or the madam or pimp she works with, these clients range from the very, very rich to a john off the street. My regular clients have always been wealthy attorneys and realtors. As a matter of fact, if it weren't for Beverly Hills/Century City lawyers and realtors, I believe some high-priced call girls' personal incomes would drop below the poverty level.

I first met "Oscar" on an assignment from Madam Alex. Oscar is one of the founding partners in a very large law firm that has grown so big that it takes up an entire floor of a very tall high-rise building on Century Park East. He is considered one of the top entertainment lawyers in town, with a clientele that includes at least a dozen Oscar, Emmy, and Grammy winners. He is also a "happily" married man and respected in the community.

On his beautiful mahogany desk is a large bowl containing hotel keys. I always wondered who he took to the hotel rooms, because what he did with me took place on a regular basis right there in his offices, with a view of the country clubs of Beverly Hills and Century City.

One of my last appointments with Oscar happened not too long ago. I was at my apartment, wondering how I was going to make my rent. Business had really dropped off after Madam Alex and Heidi Fleiss were arrested.

My telephone rang.

"Hello, Linda?"

"Yes." I recognized Oscar's secretary's voice. We've spoken many times.

"One moment for Mr. Oscar."

"Hello, Linda."

"Good afternoon, Mr. Oscar."

"I thought about you during lunch. Can you come up to discuss your *motion in limine?*"

"When?"

"As soon as you can get here."

"I can be there in an hour."

"Good. Make it sooner if you can."

At this point, I take my bubble bath, relax for ten minutes, do my hair, check my nails, put on some T-Top panties, a matching lace bra, garter belt, stockings, high heels, and a business suit. I jump into my car and drive over to the large, triangular-shaped building in Century City. My car is valet parked and I walk to the elevators designated for the upper floors of the building. I reach my destination and walk in. The secretary knows me.

"Linda. Let me ring Mr. Oscar. He's expecting you."

She rings his office, speaks softly into the small microphone strapped to her head, then tells me to go in. I walk down the long hallway, careful to hold my head high and keep my hips from swaying. I don't want to cause any undue amount of attention from workers in some of the open offices. After what seems to be a city block, I reach another secretary. She tells me I'm expected and waves me in. I open the door and close it behind me. It's my job to quietly turn the lock as I walk in, so attention won't be drawn to the noise of the lock turning at a later time. Mr. Oscar is on the phone.

"The contracts should be back to me this afternoon." He signals me over and continues to talk.

"I've added a pay-or-play clause. We'll see if they go for it." He motions for me to come behind his desk. As he talks in an animated fashion, he cradles the phone on his shoulder with one hand and unzips his pants with the other. He takes out his "offer of proof" and shows it to me.

"But I think they're bluffing. You know they want this contract," he continues as I start to play with his erection. With some clients, I might use an oil or lubricant of some kind to make the surface feel warm and sensuous, but in cases like this I must rely on my own mouth as a lubricant. Obviously, I can't eat crackers just before. I also take my lipstick off before I begin, as a courtesy. I wouldn't want to leave behind any telltale signs of my visit on the bottom of that crisp white shirt or his boxer shorts.

I proceed as if I'm having the time of my life, enjoying every lick and careful not to make any smacking noises. Oscar knows I don't make any noises that can't be explained on the other end of the line. If I did, I could kiss his business good-bye. He looks at the picture of his wife on his desk and continues with his deal-making.

"No, I'm telling you, we want to play this one close to our vest." He takes his hand, scoops up his nuts and lifts them outside of his pants. I put my hand on them and squeeze.

"We've retained the rights to ancillary markets."

By now, he's about to "close the deal." Without so much as a moan, he "executes the contract."

"Good. I'll talk with you tomorrow. Take care of that cold." He hangs up. He puts his limp penis back into his pants, jots down the elapsed time on the call sheet so he can bill the client for the phone call, and starts to dial another number. As he begins the next call, he pulls out his billfold and hands me three hundred dollars. Nice, easy, simple, and clean. He has his conscience in tack, I have my money in hand, and it's "See you later" till he calls again. Probably next week.

Meanwhile, I head several blocks away to a Beverly

Hills realtor client (married, of course) who beeped me earlier in the day. He's eager to show me something special he's just listed.

The Chances You Take

When I was young, everything seemed easier. I had too many men, too little time, and too much money. Then it all changed. The older I got, the harder it got. When you're young, men help you out of jams, pay your rent, buy you presents. The older you get, those same men are still out there looking, but the girls get younger and nobody wants to rescue the women who need to be rescued most.

I thought I had given up hooking for the last time. I had a job as a receptionist at a real estate office in Beverly Hills. The work was easy. I met a lot of people and was really settling into going straight. One night I returned home from work and found my answering machine blinking,

"Hello, Linda. A friend of mine suggested I call. I'm in from Texas and I'd like to have a drink with you." The men left his name and hotel phone number.

I was tired, and besides, I had given up hooking. I decided not to call.

About one month later the phone rang again. This time I was home and I answered the call. The mysterious voice spoke with a southern drawl.

"Hello, Linda?'

"Yes."

"This is Stanley. I'm back in town. Can you meet me for a drink?"

"How did you get my number?"

"From your boss."

I half figured my real estate boss had given out my number just to do his friend a favor. I thought about the possibilities—this man might be someone my boss genuinely wanted to fix me up with. I was single, after all. Maybe I'd meet Mr. Right.

The man continued. "Linda. Can you come over?"

"Where?"

"The Brentwood Holiday Inn. I'll meet you in the bar."

I agreed. I figured I would size him up. If he seemed like dating material, I'd act like I was on an innocent blind date. If he had trick potential, maybe I could supplement my income.

I showered and toweled off, taking stock in the mirror. I still looked great. It had been a while, but I hadn't lost it.

I showed up wearing riding britches and a preppy-looking blouse. I walked into the bar and looked around. There were no familiar faces—that was good. I noticed an attractive man at a table in the corner of the bar. He looked up at me, smiled, and signaled me over. He was wearing the blue sport coat he told me he'd have on and fit the description he'd given me. I could tell Stanley was surprised at how I looked. I realize now he was probably expecting a woman dressed in black fishnet stockings, a low-cut dress with a push up bra, and a miniskirt that barely covered her behind.

I strolled over to his table and sat down. Stanley explained that he owned a computer company and was opening an office in Los Angeles. It seemed that my boss had found some office space for him in Westwood and he was there to look it over. I listened as if I cared and then went into my background.

I did my usual ten minutes on growing up in Newport Beach and how I landed in L.A. via a scholarship to UCLA. I told him how I had wanted to become an attorney, but money was tight. It was the perfect lead in. I presented myself as a damsel in distress who needed someone to help me get my financial situation together. I said I liked working at the real estate company, but unfortunately the money wasn't very good. Voilà—he took the bait.

"Linda, do you need some money now?"

"Well, I could always use some money."

"How much would it take for you to show me a good time?"

That was what I was waiting for. I stared at him intently.

"A good time? Or a great time?" I purred.

He laughed. "I'm kind of tired, but I'll go for it. How much for a great time?"

"Three hundred dollars."

Stanley smiled, paid the bill, and within a few minutes we were in the elevator on the way up to his room.

From the moment he opened the door, I should have suspected something. The room didn't seem lived in. It was too perfect. The bed was neatly made and the bathroom was spotless, as if nobody had been there. If I had been more aware and not so fixated on that three hundred dollars, I would have gotten out of there faster than it took for Stanley to proposition me. But instead I took the money, put it on the dresser, and began to do a sensuous strip tease. Stanley seemed pleased with my slow-motion delivery. But as I reached back to unhook my lace bra and release my breasts, he suddenly flashed a badge. In minutes the room was filled with undercover officers. I was busted. My life was never the same again.

Though I plea bargained for a lesser offense, the arrest is still on my record. It reads "prostitution," even though I was promised the incident would be "taken care of." They obviously didn't keep their promise. So what else is new?

ADVICE TO YOUNG GIRLS

Who Come to Hollywood with Majestic Dreams, Beautiful Figures, and a Need to Please

I came to Hollywood fresh out of high school, with a scholarship to UCLA in hand and with hopes of a career as a successful attorney. Somewhere along the way I lost my dream, and more important, I lost my self-respect. If exposing my most intimate stories keeps one girl from traveling down the lonely path of drug addiction and prostitution, I will feel that my journey has not been wasted.

I share my stories today from a Los Angeles County halfway house in Sylmar, California. I see my life more clearly now than I ever did while looking through the drug-hazed, rose-colored glasses I used to wear. Take it from someone who thought she was on top of the world: if you're on drugs, nothing seems real, including what you see when you look in the mirror. You may be young and beautiful now, but if you take the road I took, before you know it you'll be all used up with no place to go. You'll have no life to speak of, and after frittering away hundreds of thousands of dollars you'll be unable to get a job more meaningful than selling towels at a local department store—like me.

In Hollywood, people want you when you're young and beautiful. But as the looks fade, so do the good times. I've been with CEOs of successful companies. I've dined and slept with princes and movie stars. I've shared their money, their secrets, and their sexual fantasies. And I would trade every single memory for a normal life.

As an ex–call girl who worked for both Madam Alex and Heidi Fleiss, my life may appear to have been exotic and glamorous. In reality, it has been tragic. I don't want young girls to get the message that what I've done in my life is OK. It isn't. What I'm about to say may sound like a cliché or something your parents might say, but believe me, it comes from my heart, from my experience. As I sit in jail for drug possession and breaking my probation, I've had time to ponder my life and the mistakes I've made.

First, I was too nice when it came to sharing my body. Girls are often raised to be polite, but nice girls are easy marks for anyone who wants to use and manipulate them. I can't count how many times I've given my body to a man just because he expected it, not because I wanted to. I wish I had thought about it before giving away anything so precious for mere dollars, gifts, momentary excitement, or acceptance. I wish I had learned that it's OK to disappoint your boss, your pimp, your boyfriend, or even your husband. The truth is, when sex is a condition for anything—a job, love, acceptance—the act will simply make you feel bad. It will start you down a road of self-loathing and guilt.

I remember once seeing the mother of a teenage girl who had been murdered. She looked sadly into the television camera, tears in her eyes, and said, "If I had one thing to do over again, I would have taught my daughter not to be so nice."

It took me far too long to get suspicious of things that were too good to be true. There will always be a price to pay. I've learned the hard way that only work, discipline, and persistence—and maybe a little positive visualization—will help me achieve a goal. There are no easy short cuts.

Drugs and alcohol have, of course, been my nemesis. They took over my life before I realized it. When I arrived in Los Angeles to attend UCLA as a pre-law student, drugs were my unraveling and downfall. My addiction to drugs made it harder and harder for me to get up and keep going in the direction I needed to go. Soon I was off on an entirely different path. In order to make the decisions necessary for a career and a life, you need to be clear-headed and sober. I wasn't.

Finally, I wasn't true to myself. As a young student, I had goals and dreams. I also had boundaries and limits. But I compromised my integrity, and it didn't work. Instead of the easy money I made leading to the fulfillment of my dreams, it only led to more compromises and eventually to abandoning my goals all together. I betrayed myself. I lost the strong sense of self I once had. I lost my confidence in myself. Sitting here in jail today, it is very clear to me that the ends don't justify the means. More often, if you take the wrong means to reach a goal, you will sabotage the end you desire to achieve.

I wish the script of my life had been different. I wish I had crafted it with love for myself and with care. I wish I had written out of my script people who bullied me, controlled me, put me down, or enticed me with promises of something for nothing. Now I take more careful stock of the people in my life. I try to befriend nurturing, honest people who want the best for me.

As I look back on my life, if I had stuck with my original plan, I would have been an attorney by now. Perhaps I would even be married, with children, instead of a lost little girl all grown up, searching for the dignity and independence that I gave away so willingly when I was young.

Tiffany

Tiffany

HEIGHT:	*5'11"*
HAIR:	*Ash–blonde*
EYES:	*Blue*
WEIGHT:	*128*
PROFESSION:	*Call girl*
BORN:	*Switzerland*
HOBBIES:	*Horseback riding, boating, sewing, and design-ing jewelry.*
EDUCATION:	*Boarding schools*
FIRST SEXUAL EXPERIENCE:	*At eighteen, with an older man, twenty-four, on Catalina.*
GOALS AND DESIRES:	*To be a stepmother and housewife.*
SEXUAL FANTASY:	*To be able to stay with the same person for the rest of my life and never get bored.*
DRUGS:	*Mandrex, Valium, marijuana, Quaaludes.*
HAPPIEST MEMORY:	*Walking on the cusp of a mountain near Brienz.*
WORST EXPERIENCE:	*Making the same mistake twice.*
SEX PARTNERS:	*Jack Nicholson, John Ritter, Don Simpson, and more.*

THE DIARIES

For the Record

I was born in Switzerland. I grew up around guns and military and political intrigue because of my father's work. In most ways, though, I guess I was a pretty normal kid, even though I remember being a loner and sad a lot of the time. My best friends were horses. I loved to ride and my dream was to ride in the Olympics.

Everything changed when my family moved to Los Angeles. I was a teenager and didn't know the circumstances, but I knew our family income dropped significantly. My father was quite upset about it.

As a teenager, I was a strikingly beautiful, tall, blond, blue-eyed innocent. Men would whistle at me, women would stare, and it seemed as though the world was mine for the taking. If somebody had told me then that within a few years I would become a prostitute, a drug addict, and a bondage queen with an arrest record—and that I would be a key prosecution witness testifying against Heidi Fleiss—I'd have thought them certifiably insane.

A couple of things may have planted the seeds that led me to my later profession. On one occasion I was dressed in some scanty clothing and my father saw me. "You look like a hooker," he said angrily.

"What is that?" I asked. My English wasn't very good yet and I really didn't know what the word meant. My father didn't explain it, but I would learn the meaning soon enough. Another time I met a man named Ray when I was out dancing with some friends. He asked me if I would sleep with an older man for money. I said "absolutely not." Unfortunately, that didn't prove to be the case for long.

BEVERLY HILLS, AUGUST 1990

The First Time for Money

As I look back now over the events that led to my becoming a call girl, I have to admit that I was very innocent and naive to have trusted and believed many of the people I met in Hollywood. It's not much consolation to realize that many young women like myself are being taken advantage of every day by con artists, crooks, pimps, madams, and johns.

I had designed a line of jewelry, but although I made some money from it I could never find an investor. I also was a terrific seamstress and worked in the clothing business for a while. But my great love was music. I wanted to write lyrics for songs, and I was hoping to get some connection into the music business.

One night, at a restaurant called Trumps, I met a man who I thought would help me. His name was Carl Summers. Carl had a company called Haze Music Productions. He showed an interest in me and I spent many hours hanging around his recording studio. I also did cocaine with him, up at his home on Mulholland Drive. I never saw anyone make recordings at his studio, but Carl had a lot of beautiful young girls hanging around, answering the phone. At some point Carl told me he could help me with my career, but it would cost me a consultation fee of $22,000 a year. His advice was pretty expensive, I thought. It must really be valuable. So when Nikki, one of the young girls who answered his phone, told me she knew how I could make some easy money, I decided to try it.

Nikki picked me up one evening not long after our conversation. We drove to the home of a very famous man in the entertainment industry who was a producer and an agent for high-powered actors. I was wearing the miniskirt and cotton blouse that she'd asked me to wear—an outfit that made me look like a little girl. She was very specific about exactly what the producer expected of me. All I had to do was talk like a child from the moment we entered his house. I was to pretend I was Daddy's little girl, and I had the hots for Daddy. It didn't seem so bad. After all, I thought, I'm an imaginative person with some pretty wild fantasies myself. And I'd make three hundred dollars for my appearance and my performance.

When we arrived, I was surprised to see a very handsome man, someone you wouldn't think would have to pay for anything, much less prostitutes to "perform" for him. And perform we did. We followed Daddy's orders even when it included getting down on our knees and barking like a dog and oinking like a pig.

The good news was that he paid three hundred per hour, so my take was a whopping nine hundred dollars for the evening! I almost had a heart attack, though, watching all the cocaine the producer did that first night. It must have been thousands of dollars' worth. What expensive habits the man had, what with his drugs and his sexual fantasies. I heard that he has cleaned up his act in recent times. I hope so. I'm sure he's a lot richer if he has.

Like so many other pretty young women, I went on to be taken hook, line, and sinker by Carl Summer's scam. I gave him the nine hundred bucks I made that night as a downpayment on my $22,000 consultation fee. Talk about stupid. When I think about it now, I can't understand why I didn't see through him. Hoping to make it in Hollywood, I placed my trust in a man I thought had some power and influence, but who in reality was only out to take advantage of my naiveté. The career he was helping me get into was not a career in musc, it was one in prostitution.

The other girls who were working for Haze Productions told me I was lucky because if I had a pimp or a madam, they'd take forty percent off the top of my $1,000 or $1,500 trick. At the time, it made sense. It seemed like a good deal. But my mind was clouded by drugs and by the wild unreality of the Hollywood scene. Show business is a dream factory where wealth, glamour, and fame seem just within reach if you're young and beautiful. All you need is the right agent, the right break, or the right connection. But for most of the women who strive for stardom and success, it is only a seductive, distant illusion. Within a few months of the producer job, I was a full-time hooker.

BEVERLY HILLS, Fall 1990

Walleed: Four Men and a Hooker

*O*ne night, after I had been trying to get away from the bad scene with Carl Summer, I was dead broke. I went out to the Rainbow Bar and Grill, where I met a guy named Cookie who wrote down a name and number on a piece of paper. "Call this girl," he told me. "She'll help you."

That was how I met Heidi Fleiss. When I showed up at her West Hollywood apartment, her first words to me were, "A guy who you could see might call me later. Are you available tonight?" She told me that she took forty percent and I would get sixty. While she was talking to me, she was fielding phone calls— mostly about the football game that she had bet several thousand dollars on. As I was leaving, she gave me this advice, "Whatever you do, don't work for Madam Alex."

As time went on, being a call girl became my primary profession. After I got more into it and learned my way around, I ended up working for both Heidi and Madam Alex—and sometimes for neither. There were times when I'd pick up someone on my own, a friend would call, or I'd be out at the Polo Lounge in the Beverly Hills Hotel and someone would look good to me. For these connections, I didn't feel like I owed

Heidi or Alex shit. But you take your chances in these situations. You never know what you might be getting into.

I'd met a client named Walleed through some friends. When he called me with instructions on when and where to meet him, I thought it would be a typical in-and-out deal, with maybe a nice dinner thrown into the mix. I knew the money was good. It always was with my Arab clientele.

I put on a lot of makeup and a sexy spandex body suit. I usually don't wear panties under bodysuits because the lines show. The outfit was so tight you could make out my pubic hair. Arabs like their women to be shaved all over, but that was too much for me. I've done a lot of things in my life, but I've never shaved my pubic hair.

Arabian men usually like women to be bigger than me—big hips, big thighs, big everything. They usually aren't into the tall, thin, California girl look, though there are some exceptions. What I lack in the hefty category, however, I make up for by being tall. I'm over six feet in heels, which either drives men wild or drives them nuts.

I showed up at the Beverly Hills Hotel and strolled through the entrance with head held high, ignoring the stares from the hotel help and the curious tourists. My statuesque six-foot frame moved like a gazelle through the crowded lobby. I turned to my right and walked toward the elevator. On my way up to the third floor, I opened my large beige appointment book to double check the room number. One woman in the elevator subtly elbowed her husband when he didn't take his eyes off of me.

The elevator doors opened and I turned to my left.

I knew this hotel inside and out: I'd been here many times before. I walked to the end of the hall and knocked lightly, careful not to attract too much attention. Walleed opened the door. He had a smile on his face and his bushy eyebrows lifted as his brown eyes darted from my breasts to my crotch and back again. I kissed him lightly on the cheek and entered the suite. I rested my purse and appointment book on the hallway console and walked, hips swaying seductively, into the living room area. I stopped in my tracks, in shock. Before me were three more men, all wearing *gotras* (headdresses), beards, all smiling, all pleased, all waiting to gang bang a six-foot hooker—me.

I turned to Walleed, who was behind me. "Whoa, Walleed. You didn't tell me there would be four of you."

"You want more money?"

"It's not the money, Walleed. It's just that, well, I'm not into taking on four at a time."

The most I'd ever had was two. Four men at one time was not something I looked forward to. Walleed looked puzzled.

"We're all clean."

"That's not the point, Walleed. I'm not into gang banging. Clean has nothing to do with it."

Walleed reached into his pocket and pulled out a roll of thousand dollar bills that could choke a camel. I must admit that for a fleeting moment, as he peeled off ten bills, I entertained the thought of going through with the proposal. But when I took a moment and added up the take, it would have only been a little over two thousand per man. That wasn't as tempting as I first thought. Twenty thousand, maybe. But even then, I didn't like it. I contemplated how to delicately get out of this situation. Then the solution came to me.

"I know someone who can help you out, Walleed. Her name is Heidi."

"Good. Will she take all of us on?"

"Oh no." I smiled. "She's a madam. I'm sure she knows someone who won't mind doing all four of you. Let me call."

The men were looking impatient. I noticed at least one of them move his hand down to put pressure on his rising penis. As I dialed, I thought about the "little women" these men had left at home to take care of the kids. I thought about the hours those women must spend shaving in order to please their men. I wondered what the wives would think if they knew their husbands were with a foreign woman, wanting to take turns.

"Hello, Heidi?" I didn't recognize her voice at first. I think she was high.

"Tiffany?" She knew my voice.

"I've got something for you. I'm here at the Beverly Hills Hotel with a man named Walleed—"

Heidi interrupted, "Walleed? Is that Prince Walleed?"

I turned to Walleed and asked, "Are you a Prince?"

He shook his head no.

"Wrong Walleed. But this guy is flush. He has three friends who he wants taken care of at the same time, so four total."

"So, he's looking for someone to take care of all of them?"

"Yes."

"Well, tell him I've got two girls I can send over. Do you want to take any of these gentlemen on?"

By now, I just wanted to get out of there. "No, I'm not interested," I said.

"Tell them it will be ten thousand for two girls—up front."

I relayed the information. Walleed looked over at the other men. By now, they probably would have fucked the maid, they were so horny. Walleed got their silent approval and the deal was done.

I hung the phone up and told the guys that the girls would be over within the hour. Walleed tried to talk me into staying, but just the thought of four at a time or even two of these men was too much for me mentally. I'd had enough surprises for one day. Walleed knew the rules of the game and peeled off two one-thousand-dollar bills for my trouble. In prostitution, time is money. All we have to sell is our time and our bodies. If I didn't charge when a man didn't come, couldn't come, or came too soon, I'd have been poverty stricken a long time ago.

I thanked Walleed, picked up my purse and appointment book, and was out the door.

On the way out, I went to one of the pay phones just off to the left of the Polo Lounge, opened the door, sat down, put my appointment book on the little shelf, picked up the phone, and dialed my drug connection.

AUGUST 1992

Don Simpson: An Education in Pain

A friend introduced me to Madam Alex during a
period when things were slow with Heidi. The
first thing Madam Alex asked me about was how
things were going with Heidi. The two madams were
mortal enemies ever since Madam Alex was arrested
and Heidi set herself up in competition with her, apparently stealing many of the older madam's clients.
In answer to her question, I told Madam Alex that I
didn't want to talk about Heidi with her and I
wouldn't talk about her with Heidi. She seemed
pleased with my answer but still had to vent her anger
at Heidi. She accused Heidi of not just stealing her client list but also bribing a guard to get into her storage
space and stealing priceless Dali paintings and other
art—Persian rugs and valuable antiques that Madam
Alex had placed in storage in order to hide those assets
from the IRS. As I left that first meeting with Madam
Alex she told me I had class. She knew she could get
me a lot of work. She did. Not all of her clients, however, had class.

Don Simpson, a producer known for his work on
Top Gun, *Flashdance*, and *Beverly Hills Cop*, lives in a
house on Stone Canyon in Bel Air. The white home
with green shutters is furnished in a combination of
Japanese and Italian decor. There are two Porsches in
the garage. When Don opened the door, I was surprised to see how handsome a man he was, in a rugged
sort of way. He had a flat stomach, a very sexy belly

button, and a sexy hair line that goes from his chest to his navel. The tight blue jeans that he wore were obviously chosen for the way they flatter his masculinity.

Simpson offered me a drink and talked very tenderly to me, which was not a sign of things to come. He told me he wanted to "get into my brain" and find out where I was coming from. I must admit I was taken with him, though there seemed to be a lot of psychological manipulation going on. He was very charismatic and seductive. Within a couple of hours we were in his viewing room, looking at some of his homemade video tapes. Out of the corner of his eye, he monitored my reactions as I watched.

The first tape showed Don interviewing one beautiful actress after another, after another. With each young actress, he had the same story—that he was interviewing them for a part in a movie he was making. By the end of each interview, each actress ended up having sex with him. I'm sure none of the women knew they were being videotaped. It was obvious that these girls were hoping to get a part in his movie. They were in the home of one of the most famous producers of our time, and every single one of them thought she had a chance for her big break. So off came the clothes, and each big break was actually Don's.

The third tape Don showed me that night involved a dominatrix dressed in black leather who was torturing a beautiful young girl. Both women were prostitutes, but what Don and the dominatrix did to this girl should have gotten both of them thrown into prison. Instead, it ended up in his video collection. Who knows what happened to the young girl. In the video, she was bound and tortured, tied up in bondage apparel, including a large rubber ball strapped to the girl's mouth so she couldn't scream. She was then led to the bathroom. The dominatrix, a prostitute I recognized named Patricia Colombo, forced the girl to lean over a toilet. With her head dunked in the water, the girl was told to drink. At the same time, the dominatrix had a black, twelve-inch dildo strapped to her body. She fucked the girl with it, and also put another specially designed tool up the girl's ass. Don Simpson, meanwhile, was standing over the toilet pissing into the bowl as the girl drank. It was sick, sick, sick.

Don called this way of "turning out" girls and exploring every conceivable sadomasochistic fantasy *sexual healing*. He said he was determined to "heal" people with this method. Somehow I fell under his spell. I don't even know how. At the time, I thought it made perfect sense. He had me thoroughly convinced that I was participating in his sexual healing by introducing him to girls and by participating in the S&M practices myself. By the end of our relationship, Don had me convinced I should ignore my body and any pain I might be subjected to or subject others to, per his instructions. He also told me something I remember word for word, something that seemed strange considering how he treated women. He said, "You women have no idea of the power of what you've got between your legs." It seemed odd. I looked around the world, particularly in Hollywood, and it was what men held between their legs that seemed to be the prerequisite for power.

One particular night, Don Simpson was with dominatrix Patricia and me and something possessed him to call Heidi for a third girl. When the third girl arrived, she took one look at Patricia—dressed in patent leather boots that came up to her mid–thigh, a leather studded bustier, whip, and mask—and swallowed hard. It was obvious she wasn't the S&M type. She was a virgin to these perversions, and you could tell she was scared.

Don took this innocent-looking girl upstairs to his bedroom and before too long we could hear her screaming. Patricia and I walked to the top of the stairs and listened. Don apparently heard us, threw open the door, read us the riot act, and told us to wait downstairs. About an hour later, the young girl came downstairs in tears, obviously shaken up. Don paid her the thousand dollars and told her to leave. I could tell by the look on her face that she was questioning what price she had paid to make her rent that month. She now had wounds to heal and horrific memories that would last a lifetime. After she left, Don had an evil smile on his face. He told us that he had "turned her out"—beaten her, screwed her, and introduced her to S&M for the first time. It gave Don a good deal of pleasure to take a naive young girl and do this to her.

Don Simpson's serious bondage games were like something out of Marquis de Sade. He was responsible for many destructive elements in my life and the lives of many young women who, lured by the chance to make a lot of money, enter the hell he presides over. People like Don Simpson have the luxury of being able to do to young women things that most men would go to jail for. He gets away with it because he can afford to pay for the privilege and because the atmosphere in Hollywood condones if not encourages it. And he gets away with it because women like Madam Alex, Heidi, and me are willing to go the distance to provide men like him with what they want. Other

powerful men are also into "toilet sex," and other producers take advantage of their position of power over
actresses, but I have never heard of anyone as bad as
Simpson.

Don Simpson gave me more than an education, he
gave me a new, perverse set of values, and messed my
mind up for so long I'm still recovering from his psychological programming. What he called sexual healing was nothing more than raping my mind and body
while telling me my mission was to ignore the pain.

The last time I saw Don Simpson, he was talking
about how much he hated Heidi Fleiss. I think they had
a disgreement about money. He said he wanted to have
her taken out into the desert and killed. Shortly after
this last encounter, I heard that I was added to the list
of people he wanted to have "taken care of." That
might have been more merciful than what he already
had done to me.

John Ritter: Nine and a Half Hours

I've entertained many men in my home. If my
couch could talk, it could make a lot of money
from the *National Enquirer*. I've been with famous
people, ordinary Joes, and too many strangers. Most
of the time when I bring someone home, they're interested in one thing only, and it has nothing to do with
helping me get out of my not-so-great neighborhood.
If some of the guys I've been with could have looked

past their purely physical interest in me, they'd have realized that I really needed help in getting out of where I lived.

When I met an actor named John Ritter—the son of the cowboy, actor, and singer Tex Ritter—I was living where I live now, in an unsafe neighborhood. But helping me with any of my problems never occurred to him. He was primarily interested in telling me his own. It began with an innocent flirtation.

Heidi Fleiss sent me to New York to meet with a wealthy client, an investment banker. Heidi always insisted that her girls be treated well, so I was flown first class on MGM Grand, compliments of my client. When I landed at Kennedy Airport my limo hadn't arrived, so I waited by the street in front of baggage claim. I was looking really good in my Yves Saint Laurent paisley miniskirt and velvet jacket. The bustier I wore accentuated my firm breasts. People stared at me and I was enjoying the attention.

Behind me, at a bank of telephones, I could hear a voice say, "Hey Mom, guess who's on the phone next to me? *John Ritter!* You know, from 'Three's Company!' " I turned to look. Sure enough, before me stood the same actor who starred with Suzanne Somers and Joyce DeWitt on the show about three roommates who live together in California. He was dressed to attract as little attention as possible, wearing a New York Mets baseball hat, dark sunglasses, baggy pants, and a baggy jacket. He looked over at me and shrugged his shoulders as he took the telephone from the fan who had just asked him to say hello to his mother. John kindly said hello to the apparently thrilled woman on the other end of the line. Then he handed the phone back to the impressed young man and walked away.

I continued looking for my limo. A few minutes later, John Ritter walked back toward me and walked away again—he appeared to be waiting for a ride as well. He seemed to be nervous. At some point, he came back again and initiated a conversation. He had been on the same plane as me and asked who I was. I told him I was on a modeling assignment. He told me he was here to appear on "Good Morning America" the next day. For some reason, his limo hadn't arrived. He was tired and wanted to get to his hotel and go to sleep. He hadn't slept well in a couple of days and was edgy. He excused himself and made a call, attempting to find out what happened to his ride. When my limousine pulled up, it was only natural for me to offer him a lift. He accepted gratefully.

Once inside the limo, we made small talk. John's eyes glanced down at my YSL miniskirt, so I decided to spread my legs a little and give him a thrill. I also gave my top a little tug downward, exposing the top of my nipples over so slightly. I had a captive audience. John couldn't take his eyes off of me.

But even with my seduction, his eyes began to close. I commented on how tired he looked and decided to offer him a few Xanax (an antianxiety pill that is often prescribed to help people calm down) to help him relax. He immediately knew what they were and took them, appreciating my generosity.

After John pocketed the Xanax, our eyes connected and sparks flew. We definitely made a sexual connection, but my time was spoken for and his was as well. When I dropped him off, John said he would be back in L.A. in a couple of weeks. He promised to call. I honestly didn't expect he would. He didn't know that I was a prostitute and still doesn't know unless, of course, he's reading this book. He just thought I was a beautiful woman who happened to be attracted to a famous television star. This was true, but the fact that I was an extremely high-priced call girl was also true. I went on to the Plaza Athenee Hotel to service my client. A couple of days later I flew home to Los Angeles. I thought I'd seen the last of John Ritter.

I was surprised when he actually did call a couple of weeks later. He was interested in more than finding out how my modeling assignment went. He never mentioned going out together sometime. He only said, "Can I come over and see you?" It was morning. I agreed.

When John arrived he was wearing the same New York Mets baseball hat and sunglasses he wore the day we met. He seemed pleased to see me, but the first thing he asked was, "Is this neighborhood safe?" I told him it wasn't. But like most men, he wasn't concerned enough to ask me anything about myself or why I lived in this neighborhood. He was only concerned with what I could do for him. Within thirty minutes, we were both nude.

Our lovemaking started out like any other. Then, however, we went from the usual, to the unusual, and beyond. What made this experience so different for me was the amount of time we were together having pure, hot, jackhammer sex. Minute after minute, hour after hour, it went on and on and on. John was like a hungry animal who hadn't made love in a year. He took over my body and gave it an extraordinary workout, the likes of which I'm not sure I've ever known. Nothing had ever been as unrelenting as this.

227

John apparently believed I was a struggling actress and that I was thrilled to have an opportunity to take care of the sexual needs of someone who had "made it." He kept turning me every which way but loose, riding me hard and giving me all he had. He entered every opening in my body that I would allow him to. At one point I grasped the headboard and held on tight for a ride that would have made his cowboy father proud. He beat me unmercifully with his beautiful shaped six-shooter. Like the famous sex scene from the movie *Bull Durham*, we moved around the house to the kitchen, where I braced myself between the doorway jams and did deep knee bends onto his steel rod as he lay beneath me on the cold kitchen floor. He had no idea of the value he was getting for free! For what we were doing together, professional that I was, I should have made several thousand dollars at least—and more for overtime.

Finally, after nine hours of thrusting penetration in every possible position, he was through. We lay still on the living room floor. John smiled that little boy smile and told me he was hungry. He would have been quite content for me to have taken care of his dietary needs as well as his sexual ones, but the last thing I was about to do was cook for him. I was exhausted, and besides, I didn't have any food in the refrigerator. I suggested we go to a nearby Denny's.

Denny's was filled with characters John Ritter might have wanted to portray in an acting role, but in real life it was obvious that he didn't want to associate with this kind of riff-raff. After a few minutes of paranoia about whether or not we were safe to even be here, he asked, "This is the kind of neighborhood where people get killed, isn't it?" He finally calmed

down, and after a little small talk about his upcoming
television project, he began talking about his wife. He
said he was having a lot of trouble with her because
she had found out about his mistress. His wife had told
him that if he didn't get rid of the mistress, she'd leave
him. He told me that he was still in love with his wife,
an actress named Nancy Morgan. She had been as understanding as anyone could be for years, but when
his mistress came into the picture, she finally threat-
ened to throw in the towel. Meanwhile, he said, his
love for the new mistress was making him feel like
that song, "Torn Between Two Lovers." In the end,
though, his children took priority and he wanted to
stay with his wife. I thought, so what were you doing
with me for the past nine-and-a-half hours? John
showed me pictures of his kids, then glanced at his
watch and told me he had to pick them up from school
in a little while. Finally the conversation drifted back
to his mistress again and how much he missed her
since they had broken up.

Certain men are like selfish little boys. Their only
concerns are their own needs and problems. Here I
was, a struggling "actress" who'd just given him nine
and a half hours of what had to be some of the best sex
he'd ever had. Then I had listened to his problems.
You'd think he would have wanted to see if he could
help me with my career or buy me a present or, at the
very least, ask questions about who I was and what
my life was about. He didn't do any of that. When I'm
on a job, a client will often have sex with me and then
tell me his troubles. So listening to Ritter was no different from my normal work, only this time I wasn't getting paid.

John paid the check and once again expressed his

paranoia about the neighborhood as we drove back to my place. He dropped me off and headed over to pick up his children. Within an hour or so, my doorbell rang. It was John. He had dropped his kids off and was now back for more! I couldn't believe this guy's stamina. When he was through—this round lasted about ninety minutes—he stuck around for a little while. He seemed lonely, or maybe he just didn't want to go home.

When I meet men on a nonprofessional basis, I sometimes hope for a relationship. The more I knew about John's situation, however, the more it seemed like a convoluted, complicated time in his life. From what he told me, it really didn't seem like there was room for one more, so I tried to push out any thoughts of something permanent. Besides, maybe life was imitating art here. After all those years of playing the part of Jack Tripper with two ladies on "Three's Company," maybe it was hard for him to be content with only one woman.

When John left, he didn't even say, "I'll call you sometime." I thought I'd never hear from him again. Then I ran into him one day on the set of a television show he was shooting. I had been hired for a small part on the show "Hearts Afire." I would never embarrass someone by speaking first to them in public, just in case there was someone else around who knew of my call-girl history. This self-imposed rule particularly applied to the movie stars I knew. So when I saw John on the set, I didn't say a word. It took a while for him to recognize me, but when he did, he walked over and said, "Tiffany?" Then he hugged me and acted like we were long lost friends. At the end of the day, he took me aside and whispered in my ear, "Can I come over to your house later?" I told him yes, and within the hour he was knocking on my door once again, dick in hand.

This time our lovemaking session only lasted two hours. He managed to fit in a lot of positions in that relatively short amount of time, and we added a new venue to our repertoire—the bathroom sink.

When the hot sex was over, he once again talked about his wife, his kids, and that mistress. He soon said good-bye (this time no Denny's invitation), and left. After being his sex object, counselor, psychiatrist, and acrobat, it would have been nice if he'd have at least called me sometime to say, "Hello," "Thanks," or at the very least, "What did you say your last name was?" Oh, well. After all, it does take two to Mambo.

FALL OF 1992–1994

Jack Nicholson: A Baptism

*H*ave you ever had that electric feeling of anticipation, when you know great things are about to happen? I had this feeling one night as I headed over to Heidi Fleiss's new home in Benedict Canyon for a birthday party she was throwing for Mick Jagger. I entered Heidi's house at 1270 Tower Road in Beverly Hills, and for just a moment I almost forgot that I was one of the highest paid call girls in Beverly Hills.

I glanced around the room at the many Hollywood deal-makers who were there. A producer was busy talking with the guest of honor, Mick Jagger. Mick was in fine form for a man his age. A lot of Heidi's regular clients were milling about, including Charlie Sheen. Charlie spent a lot of money with Heidi. Why not? He could afford to indulge, with his riches from hit movies like *Platoon*, *Wall Street*, *Navy SEALS*, *Hot Shots*, and *The Three Musketeers*. Charlie disappeared with one of his regulars, a girl who told me that he always gave her a tip on top of the standard two thousand dollars a pop. I don't know if it was because Charlie was good in bed, if it was the money he paid her for her services, or if it was the fact that Charlie was so famous, but she always had a smile on her face. I tried to keep track of Jagger just to see if he would be partaking of the "treats." Knowing Heidi, she'd probably be offering up at least a couple of girls to him on the house. We all knew that anything we did for Heidi, she'd repay in kind later.

Mick was still surrounded by a combination of Hollywood power brokers and hookers. Then I caught the eye of a very famous star, the man known as The Joker. We connected from about twenty feet away. It was like I had been plugged in and turned on. It was magnetic. I decided to let nature take its course. If he came over to talk, I would be happy to meet him. If he didn't, then I'd just have to admire him from a distance.

I grew up on Jack Nicholson's films: *The Last Detail*, *Carnal Knowledge*, *One Flew Over the Cuckoo's Nest*, and of course my parents' favorite film, *Chinatown*. And here was Jack Nicholson in person, staring me down. I felt a sexual tingle right to my toes. Heidi Fleiss must have noticed our connection because she walked over to Jack, took him by the arm, and walked him toward me.

"Tiffany, I'd like you to meet Jack Nicholson," Heidi smiled as she talked.

My knees became weak. I tried to keep my composure as he took my shaking hand. Another one of Heidi's girls, Peggy, walked by. Heidi grabbed Peggy by the arm, then grabbed me, and not missing a beat, she said, "Here, Jack. You can have them both, no charge."

Heidi meant sexually, of course. I felt something I rarely feel—embarrassment. Jack gave Heidi that wicked little smile of his and his two hands rose in the air with a "stop embarrassing me" gesture. He then licked his lips and started shaking his head from side to side as he looked down at his shoes. About fifteen minutes later, Jack whispered in my ear, "Let's get out of here and go to my house." And we did.

Jack's home is decorated in what I call Early Egyptian Bazaar. Everything in his house has its own personality. One table has silver plates with imprints of cows. The soft lighting spotlights an extensive art collection. He has a most unusual ashtray, with figures of women wearing nightgowns lounging elegantly on the rim. The furniture is mostly oriental antique, and his telephone rings with a soft, wind-chime sound.

Jack was a gentleman. As soon as I entered the house, he offered me a drink. He took my coat and told me I looked beautiful. It didn't take us long to make our way into the bedroom. Instinctively, I massaged his entire body. Sometimes when I'm with a man I try to be more like a geisha girl than a prostitute. The only thing on my mind is to give pure, lasting, unadulterated, unforgettable pleasure. I used my entire body that night, straddling Jack and letting my hair fall over his stomach and thighs. I let my other hair brush up against his skin as well, starting with his toes and ending with his nose. This drove him crazy. I felt like that man was born to make love to me.

Jack called me again, and again. He told me he had enjoyed our first "carnal knowledge experience" and he wanted more. How could I refuse? I knew there would not be any money in it for me, and though my rent always seemed to be due, this seemed like more of a friendship. Money might cheapen it. Besides, I've never known any really big star to pay for sex. They know they can get it for free.

The second time Jack invited me over I knew what I was in for and the nervousness was replaced by expectation. I decided to drive him wild by wearing red from head to toe. Underneath my slip dress I wore a red lace-and-satin bra, with thigh-high red stockings, a red garter belt, and a very tiny red G-string. When Jack opened the door he grinned, and I don't think that grin left his face until sometime after I left, probably days later. It was that good. At one point in the evening I said, "Jack, darling, would you please bring me one of your Oscars?"

He was taken aback at my request, but he left the room and soon returned holding an Academy Award. My arms stretched out for it. He laid the old statue into my hands and I was surprised at how heavy it was. As Jack resumed driving me to kingdom come, I caressed the heavy symbol of all that Jack was professionally.

Though he has a chef, Jack only invited me over when his help was not home. We learned a lot about each other during our six-month relationship of Sunday visits and hot sex. Jack Nicholson once talked about me in a *Playboy* magazine interview. My mother called when she'd read the article. In it, Jack describes chasing a girl around with a Ping-Pong paddle. My mom immediately asked, "What did you do to make him do that?" As open and honest as I am, I wasn't about to tell her.

My most memorable moment with Jack Nicholson occurred after a love session that lasted for hours. Jack excused himself and headed into the shower. After a few minutes, intending to join him, I entered the bathroom and headed toward the sound of the hot, running water. I opened the glass door and saw his wet body, all lathered up, and that satiated smile on his face. I kneeled on the floor of the shower, then laid face down and slowly rolled over to where my face was on the shower floor, looking up at him. As he looked down at me, I opened my mouth. It was like a choreographed mating ritual of some rare, South American animal species. We were in silent mutual agreement over what was to happen next. It was obvious to me Jack had never done this before, but he instinctively took my cue and peed into my mouth.

Being pissed on was nothing new to me. After all, Don Simpson had by now relieved himself on me more times than I'd like to recall. In the beginning, just the thought of the act disgusted me. But in time, I actually started enjoying the warm, sensuous feeling and intimacy I shared with my clients during the ever-more-popular bathroom "water sports." When Jack was through, he reached down, picked me up, and kissed my warm, wet mouth as he tasted his own urine.

Jack called me afterward and said thank you. He also asked if I enjoyed myself. In many ways, he's quite a gentleman. Although he never offered to pay me, one time he offered to pay for my cab home. But I told him, "No, I can't take money from you. It wouldn't be right." He didn't push the matter.

Jack Nicholson: Party Animal

I've always been drawn to powerful, famous people like Jack Nicholson. I think it's interesting how many people will put up with inappropriate behavior when the person dishing it out is famous. I liked Jack, however, and I felt it was an honor to be with him and have him as a friend. The only gift he ever gave me was a pair of TV glasses that enable you to lie in bed and watch television or read without having to prop up your head. That's it. It was nice of him to give them to me, I guess. They are my only tangible souvenir of those days of hot sex and drugs in a Beverly Hills mansion.

"Did your cunt make you call me?" Jack asked a young woman on the other end of the telephone line. I had been invited to his home for sex and cocaine. There was a beautiful young girl already partaking when I arrived. Jack had also invited a male friend. He frequently had at least one other man at his house, eager to share whatever Jack felt like sharing. The girl and the man were doing lines on a plate when the telephone rang. Jack often asked questions like this simply for shock value. The girl on the other end of the line gave her reply. Jack later told me that she said something like, "Oh no, I'm calling you because you're such a wonderful man and I was thinking about you." To which Jack, still smiling, responded, "If your cunt didn't make you call me, why the hell are you calling?"

Maybe this was his way of asking a third female to join the party. That would have made it nice for Jack and his friend, but the girl snorting next to me didn't seem like she wanted to share the cocaine with anybody. Her head was buried in the plate as she continued to do lines. Jack hung up the phone and came back to the party.

"Girls, girls, the cocaine won't go away. It will still be here after we've had our fun." Jack was anxious to collect for his generosity. But the other woman couldn't get enough coke. Clearly, the last thing on her mind at that moment was having sex. I, however, preferred downers to cocaine. Mexican Quaaludes were heavenly to me. Jack and I disappeared into the bedroom.

Jack was a wildman in bed that night. Then, when he was through with me, he began to slap me. Maybe it was the drugs, maybe I'd displeased him, but he hauled off and hit me hard. I kept my composure.

"Take it easy, tiger. Easy, easy." I kept repeating. He kept slapping.

Finally, he stopped. I wondered what that was all about, as I lay there staring at him. I looked at his weathered face and his lips as he gave that unconscious smacking sound he's famous for. His closed eyes opened to discover me staring at him.

"What are you looking at?"

"Jack, you look like the Devil." I knew I was playing with fire. He could have hauled off and hit me again over that one. Instead, he seemed to be lost in thought for a moment. I repeated my statement in the form of a question.

"Has anyone ever told you that you look like the Devil?"

"Yeah. Lots of people." He smiled.

I thought back to the movie, *The Shining*, where Jack played the part of a psychotic writer who terrifies his family. He looked like that character right now. My mind started drifting. I thought about how Heidi Fleiss looked an awful lot like Shelley Duvall, the lady who played Jack's wife in the movie. I felt a little like Shelley's character must have felt in the movie. I didn't know who was sleeping next to me—someone I thought I knew, or the Devil. I was used to being slapped around. I had plenty of that when I was called out on an S&M job. But this time I wasn't being paid. Besides, my Quaaludes were wearing off and I was beginning to feel the pain.

LAS VEGAS, FEBRUARY 1993

Kerry Packer: Eight Girls in a Row

One of Heidi's clients was the infamous Kerry Packer, one of the richest men in the world. He could afford anything, and he paid handsomely for the opportunity to live out his fantasies. One afternoon Heidi got a call from one of Kerry Packer's people, who put in an order for eight beautiful, long-legged, California girls—the kind he'd ordered before.

The scene was typical up at Heidi's that day. Sev-

eral girls were lounging around, some watching television, others by the pool. After the call from Packer,
Heidi got out a pad of paper and began to write as I
looked on.

"Let's see, I'll send Darcy, Kim (a girl who would
later testify in Heidi's pandering case), Samantha,
Judy, maybe Gabriella, Bobby, and . . . Nicole." Heidi
then turned to me and said, "You in, Tiffany?"

I was always up for a good time, especially with a
millionaire of Mr. Packer's caliber. I said yes. Within a
few hours, Heidi managed to make arrangements for
eight girls to gather for an adventure of the rich and
famous kind in Las Vegas, Nevada. If Robin Leach
could have covered the story, it might have gone something like this:

"We're here at Caesar's Palace, in Las Vegas, Nevada, with Mr. Kerry Packer, one of the richest men in
the world. Tonight we'll be meeting with eight ladies
of the evening that he's just flown in for his personal
pleasure from—where else—Tinsel Town! We'll see
what a mogul like Mr. Packer does to pass the time
when he's not doing megadollar deals. Will he be able
to handle all those breasts and curves? Will the man
from down under come up for air? Stay tuned as we
take you on a sexual thrill ride that only the most am-
orous rich and famous can afford."

So much for the Robin Leach fantasy. The reality
was more like this. We arrived in Las Vegas, eight gorgeous girls, each one more beautiful than the next. At
5'11" I had the distinction of being the tallest in the
group, so I could peer over the heads of the other girls
and see the impression we made. As we walked
through the casino we commanded the attention we
deserved. Even some of the dealers momentarily took

their eyes off the gaming tables and the customers they were dealing to. Beautiful girls are commonplace in Las Vegas, but eight gorgeous ladies, surrounded by Mr. Packer's security people, were not. We were treated like royalty and we loved it.

The man in charge of our entourage, Robert, saw to it that we were all gathered and escorted to wherever Mr. Packer wanted us to be. He also told us when we had free time to sunbathe or retire to our suites.

The opulence of Caesar's Palace defies description. There are three categories of people who come to Las Vegas—the working Joes, the high rollers, and the royalty. Royalty included actual royalty from around the world, as well as stupendously rich people who can gamble away millions and not blink an eye. Royalty describes a person like Kerry Packer, who gambles with fifty-thousand-dollar chips as if they were Monopoly money.

One evening after a day at the pool, Robert told us we would all be dining with Mr. Packer. We were excited, to say the least. Each of us was dressed in clothing purchased at the hotel stores earlier that day; high-heeled pumps, sexy, slinky, oh-so-revealing dresses. Some of us had our hair and nails done in the beauty shop and we all looked luscious, like a *Playboy* centerfolds reunion.

Once we were gathered together, Mr. Packer's private security men, walkie-talkies in hand, escorted us downstairs to a private dining room complete with a gaming table. Mr. Packer was dressed impeccably. His manicured hand extended to greet each one of the girls. He seemed pleased with how we all looked. When we were seated, he asked us how our gambling was going and if we were enjoying our stay. We told him how thrilled and excited we were to be there, and how we looked forward to showing him our gratitude.

The waiters and security guards hovered around our host, awaiting his orders. When the dinner ended, Mr. Packer moved the entire entourage to the private gaming table where, with those fifty-thousand-dollar chips, he proceeded to lose over one million dollars— but who's counting? Though not devastated over the loss, Mr. Packer obviously wasn't in the mood for sex after the event. After saying something to Robert, he disappeared from the room without even a good-bye. Robert quickly informed us that we had been given the night off to do whatever we desired. He also handed us each a five-thousand-dollar tip.

Most of the girls gathered in one of our hotel suites and Darcy chimed in about how we shouldn't tell Heidi about the tip, fearing we'd have to pay her forty percent. The mood slowly turned from eight girls having fun to eight bitches protecting their own.

Some of the girls may have made extra money that night with some impromptu clients picked up in the casinos. I really don't know, but what I do remember is that somewhere around the third day of our stay, we all heard the Los Angeles riots had started over the acquittal of the four Los Angeles policemen in the Rodney King beatings. Suddenly we were no longer ladies of leisure having fun on a vacation. Instead, we were glued to the television sets in our rooms (two girls to a room), each wondering what we'd be coming home to, looking to see if the riots would spill over into our neighborhoods. Caesar's Palace doubled its security that night, fearful that riots might break out in Vegas. One thing is for sure, all of us felt grateful to be spending this uncertain time in Las Vegas under the protection of billionaire Kerry Packer. We felt a sense of security, and eventually camaraderie, that poured over into our dinner that evening.

Robert had instructed us that we'd all be going to Benihana of Tokyo for dinner, over at the Las Vegas Hilton. We were relieved to have the break from watching our city burn on television. The images were disturbing to us all, especially since we knew that eventually this fantasy would end and we'd be returning home to our riot-torn city.

Once again, as we paraded through the casino to the front of the hotel to our awaiting limos, the passers-by stared at us, whispering, "They look like models." Or, "They must be actresses." Somehow, nobody said, "Look at the whores. Wonder who hired them." If they did say it, it wasn't to our faces.

That night one of the girls decided to sell speed to any of us who wanted it. This was not a very smart idea, but brains were not always an abundant commodity with Heidi's girls. Perhaps Mr. Packer got wind of what was going on. The next day at the pool, Robert told us that Mr. Packer had enjoyed our company and we were all free to go home. He then arranged to meet each of us and pay us any money due. My total take for the four-and-a-half-day experience was $9,500. We all felt good about the money, but not at all happy about the prospect of returning to the real world, and a city on fire.

WEST HOLLYWOOD, SPRING 1992

That Seagram's Man

*P*eople who think prostitutes always get paid for what they do are mistaken. Sometimes we get stiffed in more ways than one. One such time I was sent on a bondage assignment with one of Heidi's regulars, an extraordinarily wealthy man. Heidi told me to stop by the Pleasure Chest and pick up a "bondage and discipline" outfit for this job. The client was an upper-echelon executive of Seagram's, the liquor company. I was also instructed to bring two hits of ecstasy, an eight–ball of cocaine, and some sleeping pills. This was a rather large drug order for only one client, but Heidi assured me that he was special and could more than afford the tab.

Wearing a sexy black spandex dress, black stockings, a garter belt, and a black leather g-string, I headed over to the Pleasure Chest. I picked out a $1,500 bondage outfit. Heidi didn't tell me whether the outfit was for me or the client, so I chose to buy a leather outfit for a man, with face hood and zippers at the mouth, eyes, and nose. I must say, I smiled at the idea of putting this macabre clothing on my successful corporate client. With my large shopping bag loaded with these goodies, I headed over to the Four Seasons Hotel on Doheny Drive.

The doormen gave me a look as I entered the hotel. In the interest of discretion, I had been instructed to get the room in my name—my client would be up shortly. This gave me time to strip down to my leather

G-string and black leather bra. When Mr. Corporate America knocked on the door, I was ready for him. Without saying a word, he looked the room over, checking to see if there were any bugging devices planted. He was quite paranoid. Next, he asked if I brought the drugs. I took out the cocaine, ecstasy, and sleeping pills and laid them on the coffee table. After getting some wine from the minibar, he proceeded to snort some coke.

This heavy-set man seemed to be whacked out from the start. It was obvious to me that he was keeping his high going, and that it had begun much earlier in the day. The next drug he took was ecstasy. The sleeping pills he would save for later, when he wanted to come down. Once he was sufficiently flying, he asked if I brought the bondage gear. I said yes, and started to unpack. If I'd had a camera, I would have taken a picture of his face when I opened up the shopping bag and took out the leather outfit. It took a second for it to register that the clothing was for him. With wide eyes and a jaw that was by now on the carpet, he retrieved his composure and said, "Ah, let's go downstairs for a drink." I was surprised, but I knew I had to give the customer what he wanted. I never complain or question, and that's why I've always been in such demand.

Then, just as we were about to leave the room, the Seagram's man suddenly unzipped his fly, took out his penis, and jacked off onto the rug! I was surprised, to say the least. He had a professional in the room with him—why was he taking things into his own hands? I thought it was rude of him to do such a thing. But then again, I was about to tie him up and beat him, so who was I to think him rude?

244

The bar was practically empty. We ordered some salmon appetizers and he launched into something prostitutes hear almost on a daily basis: "What is a beautiful girl like you doing in this business?" I told him I was an actress who always wanted to be a writer and happened to get into this for the extra money.

"You're nothing like I expected," he said. "I wanted a dominatrix who would disgust me, someone who would make me sick to my stomach to have to be with. But you, you're gorgeous."

I should have figured out then and there that I was being set up to be stiffed. But when he talked about his friend David paying me the five thousand dollars plus expenses, I thought we'd soon be heading back upstairs. I'd be his dominatrix, put him in bondage, and get paid. I never expected what happened next. He excused himself to go to the bathroom and headed out the door. After waiting forty minutes for him to return, I finally called Heidi Fleiss and told her what happened. She really freaked.

"Get your ass out of that hotel. Maybe you're being set up."

That didn't sound right. If I were being set up, it wouldn't be over salmon in the hotel bar—a cop would have kept me up in the room until the officers arrived. I asked Heidi how I was going to get paid for my time and for the outfit and drugs I bought.

"Never mind! Get the hell out of there!"

"What about the outfit? It's still in the room."

"Leave it, damn it! Just get out now."

I was never reimbursed for the hotel, the outfit, the drugs or even the salmon appetizers. I felt like a chump. Did Heidi think I was stupid? I know the rules. If a john comes, whether it's by jerking off or not, he owes the money for the session. Heidi would never let him get away with what he did. To this day I believe Heidi was paid for my time. This was the first mark against Heidi, and one reason I began to think that she deserved to go to jail.

Taking Down Heidi Fleiss

*S*ome say that I was a big part of Heidi Fleiss's downfall. It's true that I was one of the lead witnesses in the case against her, but I feel like she asked for what she got. I was only one of many people she screwed. Instead of licking my wounds, rolling over, and playing dead, however, I turned state's evidence against her.

It began with me drag-racing in Beverly Hills with a suspended license. I'll never forget the blue lights flashing in my rear-view mirror. My heart sank as I pulled over. My unpaid traffic fines and failure-to-appear warrants were about to land me in the Beverly Hills Jail.

The evening had begun with me dressing in a sexy, tight fitting, low-cut leopard print dress for my hot date with Keith Zlomsowitch. I'd met Keith in Aspen a few weeks earlier. Keith would later become known to the world as one of Nicole Brown Simpson's ex-lovers, but at this time he was my lover—and a good one. Keith had invited several people for drinks at Mezzaluna, where he was the manager. Those present included Faye Resnick (who would eventually write the best-selling book, *Nicole Brown Simpson: The Private Diary of a Life Interrupted*). When we'd finished our drinks I left, kissed Keith good-bye, and told him I'd call him later. I got into my car and soon made a big mistake, one I would relive again and again in my mind.

The stoplight was red. Wilshire Boulevard was practically empty. The guy in the Mustang next to me began to rev his engine. I knew immediately that my 350 horsepower Corvette would give him a run for his money. The light turned green and the race began. I won, but within the hour I found myself in the Beverly Hills Jail holding cell, staring my past in the face. I had been handcuffed, booked, and thrown in the "glamour slammer" because of seven thousand dollars in fines and failure-to-appear warrants.

My first call was to Keith Zlomsowitch. Lucky for me, he was home. I asked him to get in touch with Heidi Fleiss and explain my situation. I figured Heidi would help me get out. I'd done a lot for her, and besides, isn't that what madams are supposed to do—help their girls get out of jail? I settled into the modern stainless steel holding cell with three other inmates. I'd be out of this place in no time. Heidi would make sure of that.

But no one came to help. The next day I was transferred downtown to the Sybil Brand Institute for Women, part of the Los Angeles jail system. I had been chained with four other girls during our first transport. Still dressed in my sexy leopard dress, we were put in a black and white police bus with twenty-eight men. The men—many of them murderers and rapists—were, thankfully, behind a glass partition.

Once in the jail I was subjected to the usual strip search, which includes bending over, spreading my cheeks and coughing in order to dislodge any hidden drugs. A couple of the girls in the slammer had intentionally gotten arrested so that once they were inside they could retrieve condoms filled with drugs that had been shoved way inside each other's asses. They intended to sell them to incarcerated women. Their pimps had devised the plan. I felt lucky that I had Heidi, an advocate who wasn't interested in exploiting me the way these low-class whores had been. I was connected, I was in a different league. Heidi would make sure I got out of this place ASAP. Right? Wrong. The only thing Heidi did for me was to tell Keith, "Fuck Tiffany." *Fuck Tiffany*. Those were two words Heidi would live to regret having said.

Meanwhile, I had learned that another of Heidi's girls, Judy Geller, had been talking to the police about Heidi. She was bitter because at the age of thirty-two she was considered too old and wasn't getting requested by clients. She was not a happy camper and she deeply resented Heidi, by now a very wealthy and arrogant madam to the stars. Judy would eventually be one of the most important prosecution witnesses against Heidi. After Heidi's sincere concern over my well-being, I decided I'd participate in her downfall. After I got out of jail, Judy put me in touch with two men from the Beverly Hills NARCO administration vice squad, Sammy Lee and Steve Miller. We talked. Before the police were through, Heidi would not be selling drugs or bodies for a long time.

Tiffany

Lessons

*I*t all started for me when a man gave me three hundred dollars for sex. It felt good at the time. It was quick, easy money. I was actually paid for something I had readily done before for free. I felt like I had something of value. I was completely unaware of the effects prostitution would ultimately have on me, but after my first few tricks I knew I was getting sucked into a bad situation. Even then, I felt filthy.

From there it wasn't long before my introduction to drugs and full-on prostitution with Heidi Fleiss. I rode the roller coaster high, until I took a ten-story fall, with Heidi's arrest—which I helped to bring about. Suddenly my income dropped to nothing. Times were very difficult, yet to this day I know I did the right thing.

Hollywood is an exciting place. But to have a fighting chance to survive, you need to keep your wits about you and play the game from a position of control over your own mind, body, soul, spirit, and destiny. If you don't, you can end up like so many young women I know, addicted to drugs and looking to prostitution to support your habit.

When people have promised me the sun and the moon, I've had to learn the hard way that it's unlikely I will get them. Now I try to figure out what they're looking for—they may end up wanting Jupiter and Venus in return.

Another painful lesson I learned was that people

who acted like I was the greatest thing since the universe began often didn't bother to say hello once they finished using me. I've been lucky to have the friendship of some terrific people, and for that I am grateful. Others, who don't take my calls anymore, are probably taking calls from the new batch of hopeful starlets. And friends like that I can certainly do without.

I look at life as a learning experience. But in my short life, I've learned too many lessons from too many people. Some of them, I'd rather forget. Don Simpson taught me a lesson about pain—the pain I received when I was in bondage and the pain I felt internally while performing sadistic acts on others, at his behest. Eventually, I learned the lesson he wanted me to: ignore the pain. The only problem was that when I deadened those feelings, other feelings died along with them. I believe I've all but lost the ability to feel joy—or guilt.

I used to feel guilty about the fact that I brought three girls into prostitution who more than likely would never have been there if it weren't for me. One of them, Kiki, wanted to be a stripper.

"Kiki, why be a stripper for $75 a night?" I said. "You loose all self-esteem, dancing nude up there on a stage for everyone to see. If you become a prostitute, you do what you do behind closed doors, and the chances of keeping your profession anonymous are greater. Not to mention the money is good. With what you make in one hour you could pay your rent, and more."

Looking back on it now, I realize that it's a shame Kiki listened to me. She and I had good times together, but she got in way over her head. She isn't the person she was when she began. For that matter, neither am I. If I could feel guilty or sadness or pain over having turned her out, I'd at least feel more human. But I can't really feel anything anymore. Not even remorse.

Jennie Louise Frankel and Terrie Maxine Frankel are authors known for covering the Hollywood scene. Terrie Maxine is the co-editor of *Tales From the Casting Couch* and she and Jennie Louise contributed several stories to *Unfinished Lives*.

Joanne Parrent is the co-author of *Life After Johnnie Cochran*. She is also a screenwriter for feature films and television. She has written several episodes of *Dr. Quinn Medicine Woman*. She has also written for *Ms.* magazine and lectured on women's rights nationwide.

Dr. Lois Lee is the Founder and Executive Director of Children of the Night.